26889

Mrs. Ray Morgan

Bought at w.m.u day
at Jonothan creek
July 14th 1946

The Woman's Missionary Union
Program of a Church

The Woman's Missionary Union Program of a Church

by Marie Mathis and
Elaine Dickson

Convention Press

NASHVILLE   TENNESSEE

© 1966 • Convention Press
Nashville, Tennessee

5120-09

Code Number: Church Study Course
This book is number 2009 in Category 20, section
for Adults and Young People

Library of Congress catalog card number: 66-19012
Printed in the United States of America
30. MH 66 R.R.D.

About the Authors

MARIE MATHIS serves as director of the Promotion Division of Woman's Missionary Union, auxiliary to the Southern Baptist Convention, Birmingham, Alabama. She is a native of Wichita Falls, Texas. She is the widow of R. L. Mathis and has one daughter, Mrs. Cleo Coffey, Jr. Mrs. Mathis attended Midwestern College and Southern Methodist University. Hardin-Simmons University conferred the L.H.D. degree upon Mrs. Mathis in 1955. She holds the LL.D. degree from Mary Hardin-Baylor College, which was conferred in 1955. She was the first woman to receive an honorary degree from these two institutions, and is listed in *Who's Who of American Women* and *Who's Who in the South and Southwest*.

Mrs. Mathis served Texas Woman's Missionary Union as youth secretary (1938–1944), as executive secretary (1945–1948), and as president (1949–1955). While serving as president of Texas WMU, she was on the staff of First Baptist Church, Dallas, Texas, as director of church activities (1948–1952). Since 1952 she has been a member of the Baylor University administrative staff, serving as director of the Student Union Building.

Mrs. Mathis was elected president of Woman's Missionary Union, SBC, in 1956 and served in this position until 1963. At the 1963 meeting of the Southern Baptist Convention she was elected second vice-president of the Convention, the first woman to be elected as an officer in the Convention's one hundred and eighteen-year history. In 1963, Mrs. Mathis joined the staff of Woman's Missionary Union, SBC, in the position she now holds.

Mrs. Mathis is treasurer of the Women's Department of the Baptist World Alliance and is a member of the Baptist World Alliance Executive. In 1965, she was elected a vice-president of the Baptist World Alliance Executive Committee. She has served on numerous boards and committees of the Convention.

ELAINE DICKSON serves as assistant to the director of the Promotion Division of Woman's Missionary Union, SBC, Birmingham, Alabama. She is the daughter of Mr. and Mrs. John A. Dickson and is a native of Grand Tower, Illinois. She received the B.S.

degree from Southern Illinois University, attended graduate school at Illinois State University, and received the M.R.E. degree from Southwestern Baptist Theological Seminary, Fort Worth, Texas.

Miss Dickson taught at Moore High School, Farmer City, Illinois (1949–1952). She served as interim youth secretary for Oklahoma Woman's Missionary Union during the summer of 1956, and as YWA director for Texas WMU (1956–1958). She served as WMS promotion associate on the staff of Woman's Missionary Union, SBC (1958–1965) until she assumed her present position in 1965

Preface

THIS BOOK PRESENTS the current concepts of Woman's Missionary Union work in a church. In writing the book, the authors have respected the historical viewpoints of WMU while expressing the WMU program of a church in a new context—a context of cooperative planning and correlated endeavor. The book is designed for use by a pastor and church staff and by members of a church council, as well as by WMU leaders and members.

Many persons have contributed to this book. The purpose and work of an organization are always the product of many minds and hearts. The authors are indebted to leaders, past and present, who have forged the concepts expressed in this book.

Alma Hunt, executive secretary of WMU, made a significant contribution to the book. Betty Jo Corum, director of WMU editorial services, and Billie Pate, director of WMU field services, helped by evaluating each draft of the manuscript as it was written. Other members of the WMU Promotion Division, as well as state WMU leaders, made suggestions which improved the book.

The authors are particularly indebted to Beverly Goss for her assistance in research, to Betty Jo Corum for preparing the questions on each chapter and the teacher's helps at the end of the book, and to the editorial assistants and secretaries in the Promotion Division who assumed heavy responsibilities in preparing the manuscript.

MARIE MATHIS
ELAINE DICKSON

Contents

Church Study Course

THE CHURCH STUDY COURSE began October 1, 1959. It is a merger of three courses previously promoted by the Sunday School Board —the Sunday School Training Course, the Graded Training Union Study Course, and the Church Music Training Course. On October 1, 1961, the Woman's Missionary Union principles and methods studies were added.

The course is fully graded. The system of awards provides a series of five diplomas of twenty books each for Adults or Young People, two diplomas of five books each for Intermediates, and two diplomas of five books each for Juniors.

The course is comprehensive, with books grouped into twenty categories. The purpose of the course is to help Christians to grow in knowledge and conviction, to help them to grow toward maturity in Christian character and competence for service, to encourage them to participate worthily as workers in their churches, and to develop leaders for all phases of church life and work.

The Church Study Course is promoted by the Baptist Sunday School Board, 127 Ninth Avenue, North, Nashville, Tennessee 37203, through its Sunday School, Training Union, Church Music, and Church Administration Departments; and Woman's Missionary Union, 600 North Twentieth Street, Birmingham, Alabama 35203; and by the respective departments in the states affiliated with the Southern Baptist Convention. A description of the course and the system of awards may be found in the leaflet "Trained Workmen," which may be obtained without charge from any one of the departments named.

A record of all awards earned should be maintained in each church. A person should be designated by the church to keep the files. Forms for such records may be ordered from any Baptist Book Store.

Requirements for Credit in Class or Home Study

IF CREDIT is desired for the study of this book in a class or by home study, the following requirements must be met:

I. IN CLASSWORK

1. The class must meet a minimum of seven and one-half clock hours. The required time does not include assembly periods. Ten class periods of forty-five minutes each are recommended. (If laboratory or clinical work is desired in specialized or technical courses, this requirement may be met by six clock hours of classwork and three hours of supervised laboratory or clinical work.)

2. A class member who attends all class sessions and completes the reading of the book within a week following the last class session will not be required to do any written work for credit.

3. A class member who is absent from one or more sessions must answer the questions (pp. 110 ff.) on all chapters he misses. In such a case, he must turn in his paper within a week and he must certify that he has read the book.

4. The teacher should request an award for himself. A person who teaches a book in the section for Intermediates or Juniors (any category) or conducts an approved unit of instruction for Nursery, Beginner, or Primary children will be granted an award in category 11, Special Studies, which will count as an elective on his own diploma. He should specify in his request the name of the book taught, or the unit conducted for Nursery, Beginner, or Primary children.

5. The teacher should complete the "Request for Book Awards —Class Study" (Form 150) and forward it within two weeks after the completion of the class to the Church Study Course Awards Office, 127 Ninth Avenue, North, Nashville, Tennessee 37203.

II. IN HOME STUDY

1. A person who does not attend any class session may receive credit by answering all questions for written work as indicated

in the book (pp. 110 ff.). When a person turns in his paper on home study, he must certify that he has read the book.

2. Students may find profit in studying the text together, but individual papers are required. Carbon copies or duplicates in any form cannot be accepted.

3. Home study work papers may be graded by the pastor or a person designated by him, or they may be sent to the Church Study Course Awards Office for grading. The form entitled "Request for Book Awards—Home Study" (Form 151) must be used in requesting awards. It should be mailed to the Church Study Course Awards Office, 127 Ninth Avenue, North, Nashville, Tennessee 37203.

III. CREDIT FOR THIS BOOK

This book is number 2009 in category 20, section for Adults and Young People.

The Woman's Missionary Union
Program of a Church

Introduction

WOMAN'S MISSIONARY UNION has produced this concept book on the WMU program of a church to interpret understandings of WMU work in relationship to the total church program. It is the first book written from this perspective by WMU. Other church program organizations—Sunday School, Training Union, Brotherhood, Music Ministry—have produced concept books. Together the books reflect the progress of these organizations toward correlation and coordination.

Churches have been voicing the need for correlation and coordination since 1923. In that year the Southern Baptist Convention, in an effort to eliminate needless duplication and overlapping of programs in the churches, elected a committee to work on correlating and defining the work of the various Convention agencies.

In 1924 the committee reported. It recommended no changes in the organizational structure of the Convention. It did, however, recommend the reassignment of some agency responsibilities. Also it recommended that the Convention and Woman's Missionary Union each appoint members to a joint committee to work toward "closer cooperation and a clearer understanding" between Woman's Missionary Union and the Convention.

During the next thirteen years the churches kept before the Convention the need for correlation and coordination. The year 1937 marked the beginning of more intensive effort to achieve correlation and coordination. In that year the

Convention adopted a resolution which brought into existence the Southern Baptist Convention Committee on Coordination and Correlation. The committee undertook extensive study, and its findings were significant. The first finding of the committee is a point of reference for contemporary programing by church organizations: that the church itself should be recognized as central and supreme; and that all organizational loyalty should be thought of as service by the church organizations, through the church, to the kingdom of God and the world.

The other findings of the committee gave grateful recognition of the value of the existing agencies and the services which they render and pointed out the widely expressed desire for correlation and coordination, the need for a clear definition of the specific functions of the existing church organizations, and the tremendous enlistment task of the church organizations.

The Southern Baptist Convention in 1938 approved five recommendations from the Committee on Coordination and Correlation. One recommendation called for Sunday School, Training Union, Woman's Missionary Union, and Brotherhood to meet as soon as possible and thereafter at least once a year for conference and cooperation. This was the idea from which the Inter-Agency Council later emerged. The committee also recommended to pastors and churches a church council to formulate and integrate a comprehensive program, to devise a calendar of activities, to coordinate the work of all church organizations, and to discover and develop needed workers and leaders.

The Convention avoided consolidation of agencies. Rather, the Convention felt that correlation and coordination among agencies would assure vitality and uniqueness in its programs and at the same time would eliminate duplication and overlapping.

In 1940 the committee reiterated its premise that the

responsibility for correlation and coordination rested on two levels: On the agencies rested the responsibility for correlating programs, and on the churches rested the responsibility for correlating organizational leadership and expressional activities.

During the next few years the subject of correlation and coordination was submerged as World War II became the focus of attention. But the idea survived the war years, and discussion on the subject was revived.

The Committee on Church Organizations was appointed in 1946 and continued its work through the 1950 meeting of the Convention.

The committee gave all Southern Baptist pastors an opportunity to contribute to the work of the committee through a survey. Out of the survey the committee reported its findings. The first finding was that few pastors wanted radical change in the form of church organizations, although they did point out that the demands of the organizations were too burdensome.

This committee pointed to the need for:

1. *Programing:* "Activities and objectives of the several organizations are not sufficiently defined."
2. *Cooperative planning and a church program guide:* "Overwhelmingly the pastors voted for the suggested 'Guides'—curriculum, activities, leadership, stewardship, and finance—to be prepared jointly by the leaders of the several organizations."
3. *Inter-Agency Council:* ". . . the pastors expressed the wish that representatives of the several boards and institutions get together to discuss the problems involved and arrive at conclusions and ways and means of implementing them whereby better coordination and correlation could be effected."

This committee pointed to a gratifying development of

the increasing use of the church council. It foresaw the contemporary framework of organizational planning on two levels: the meeting together of leaders at denominational headquarters and of leaders in the churches for prayerful working out of problems, and the enthusiastic projecting of both tested and proposed programs for the achievement of maximum results.

This committee brought again to the Convention the proposal that there be a joint meeting of the Training Union, Sunday School, WMU, and Brotherhood agency leaders, and it added the educational departments of the mission boards.

The Committee on Church Organizations presented significant recommendations in 1948:

That the educational and mission agencies establish organizational patterns for different sized churches and that these be incorporated in printed guides.

That an all-church study course be established.

That plans and calendars of activity be correlated before publication, combining meetings wherever possible.

That the agencies formulate a uniform and flexible plan of stewardship-financing for the churches and that this plan be promoted by the agencies.

By the time the committee made its 1949 report to the Convention, it had begun to see that the problem was organizational and related to the nature of the agencies themselves. It recognized that functionally the committee was not in a position to attack and solve the problem. It encouraged in every way "initiative and responsibility on the part of representatives as teamworkers in formulating policies and plans." The shift in emphasis was from the churches to the agencies and underscored the need for the Inter-Agency Council.

The following year, 1950, the Committee on Church Organizations, in bringing its final report, cited certain evidences of progress which had been made or were to be forthcoming: church guidebook, the correlated church study course, promotion of the church council, united educational promotion of the denominational program, and the Inter-Agency Council.

These evidences of progress came slowly and with the aid of other Convention action. In 1956 the Committee on Total Program was authorized. As a result of its report in 1959, the Southern Baptist Convention voted that an organizational manual should be prepared. This manual was to contain clear-cut explanations of the programs of each of the agencies, along with the history of why the agency was formed, its biblical basis, and its reason for existence. This action by the Convention has proved to be a major turning point in Southern Baptist life. Since 1959, the agencies have been seeking to define their programs with the assistance of the Program Committee of the Executive Committee of the Southern Baptist Convention.

In 1959, the Education Division of the Baptist Sunday School Board took the initiative in studying and searching for an organizing principle which would enable personnel to plan a correlated and coordinated program for the churches. From this study, church functions were identified and church tasks were stated. The study group also discovered principles which can guide correlated planning. This research has been made available to all program leaders and has been the basis for study by personnel of all agencies responsible for church programs. The book *A Church Organized and Functioning* by Howse and Thomason expresses many of these basic concepts.

The research of the Education Division of the Baptist Sunday School Board was used by the Southern Baptist Convention in planning the annual emphases for 1964-68.

During this period a function of the church has been featured each year: to worship, to proclaim, to educate, to minister.

Since 1961, the Inter-Agency Council's Coordinating Committee has made steady progress toward correlation and coordination by improving communications among Convention agencies. The Council has become the hub of the wheel of correlation and coordination of Convention programs. Program planning and execution is being done by each Southern Baptist agency in line with its program assignment.

In accordance with 1962 Convention action, the Sunday School Board, Woman's Missionary Union, and Brotherhood have been working together in consultation with other Southern Baptist agencies to make available correlated materials and program suggestions to churches.

The future holds great potential for churches and for the denomination. Woman's Missionary Union is committed to the belief that the church is central in all planning. Woman's Missionary Union is also committed to cooperative planning which properly relates organizations of the church to work together in harmonious action to help a church fulfil its mission.

ALMA HUNT
Executive Secretary
Woman's Missionary Union, SBC

CHAPTER 1

1

Responding to the Commission

A COMMISSION echoes through the centuries, transcending time and outliving all eras. The world changes, civilizations flourish and fall, but this commission is constant and contemporary: "Go ye therefore, and teach all nations, baptizing them in the name of the Father, and of the Son, and of the Holy Ghost: teaching them to observe all things whatsoever I have commanded you: and, lo, I am with you alway, even unto the end of the world" (Matt. 28:19–20).

Christ's commission is a call to action. It is a mandate with a world scope—all nations, even unto the end of the world. It is no small enterprise that Christ projects. The mission he describes is the most demanding venture that has ever captured the imagination. Christ, who commissioned his church and gave his followers their marching orders, described his work in the world in such terms that no one can doubt how he felt about it. The contemporary challenge is as exacting as the original one: The church must be able to take hold of its mission on Christ's scale—giving the gospel to the world.

Woman's Missionary Union is a church organization committed to helping a church achieve its full potential in proclaiming the changeless gospel to a rapidly changing world.

I. A CHURCH AND MISSIONS

A church is a fellowship of baptized believers who have voluntarily joined together in covenant fellowship for worship, study, mutual discipline, Christian service, and the spread of the gospel at home and abroad.

In establishing his church, Christ appointed it as the agency for achieving God's purpose of redemption for the world. The church is a witnessing fellowship, declaring what God has done through Jesus Christ to save all men. Through the church God's eternal plan for redeeming the nations is to be realized. The late W. O. Carver, who taught missions at Southern Baptist Theological Seminary, explained that between the lost world and the kingdom of God the Lord placed the church as the medium through which the saved labor for the salvation of the world. Every congregation of baptized believers is a channel of God's redemptive purpose. Within the limits of its ability and range of influence, a church is a responsible body of witnesses charged with making the truth of God known to the whole world.

A church should be not only a witnessing fellowship but also a worshiping, learning, and ministering fellowship. Through worship a church encounters God, recognizes his holiness and majesty, and responds in loving obedience to his leadership. As a church learns, it grows in knowledge and acceptance of the Christian faith and life. As a church ministers, it makes loving response to the needs of persons in the name of Jesus Christ.

One church stated as its objective: to seek to maintain a right relationship to God through Jesus Christ, and to seek to bring all men into this same relationship. This could possibly be the objective of every church.

Each church must measure itself in terms of its relationship to a world task. Congregations must discern what God is doing in the world and must share his work in it. Every church must start where it is and ultimately expand its horizon until it includes the whole world within the scope of its interest and concern. A church's neighborhood and the world's frontier are both to be considered in a church's purpose and plans. The whole world should be in a church's census. A church must catch the heartbeat of the world's uneasy masses and do something about their needs.

Every church, regardless of its size or situation, has a response to make to the challenge of world missions. The question is not whether the response is great or small according to the standards of men but whether it contributes to winning the world to Christ. In an age of rapid change, the finest response of every church must be called forth. God waits and the world waits for this caliber of dedication. The missionary enterprise is not something in which a church may or may not engage. A church which does not share in the missionary enterprise makes a self-indictment that it does not believe in Christ as the universal Saviour and Lord or accept his Great Commission.

The church penetrates wherever missionaries go. And the truth the missionary teaches remains even when he is removed from the scene. The Bible, as it is carried around the world, is the means whereby men of every nation and kindred and tongue can hear of the wonderful works of God. It is time for churches to make full use of every means available to "send the word" to the world. Doors that open to missionaries often close, but God has said that "the light shines on in the dark, and the darkness has never quenched it" (John 1:5, NEB).

Churches are probably more able to play a decisive part in the missions movement today than at any other time in history, for they hold a unique position. A church today faces a world different from the world in which the first-century church lived and worked. A radically new setting is provided for the Christian task in today's world. A concerned church seeks to understand this "new world" and to anticipate its determinative forces.

Churches face a world torn and divided, a world commanding attention. Improved means of communication transmit news of tensions and suffering in the remotest corners of the earth. Nations are more interdependent than ever before in the history of the world. What happens in China or Africa or the United States can no longer be of passing interest; it affects profoundly the lives of world citizens. Peoples of the world are so interrelated that problems in distant countries affect not only the mind and heart but also one's mode of living. The eye and ear cannot escape reports of famines, plagues, bitter wars, earthquakes, and disasters. Headlines scream the news; television brings stark reality to the living room. Even the most insensitive person must eventually admit, "These are concerns of mine"!

The world is fearful of nuclear warfare. Any misjudgment on the part of world leadership could plunge the world into unprecedented crisis. Because of this possibility, it is urgent that the gospel be shared now. People are willing to listen. It is, therefore, the responsibility of Christians to make Christ known to all men.

In today's world a new sense of urgency is confronting the cause of missions. The spread of the gospel requires haste. God is showing his churches a new vision in the unfolding events of the present. He is calling Christians again to the fundamentals of their faith and a renewal of concern for missions. He is thrusting Christians out into places which have been comfortably ignored.

In the early centuries of Christianity the concept of world conquest captured the imagination of Jesus' disciples. The gospel spread as ordinary believers went everywhere preaching the word. Early Christians had a personal experience with Christ to share, and they shared it. On the day of Pentecost, and thereafter, believers testified concerning their experiences with their Lord, even when knowledge of their allegiance to him meant persecution and death. Stephen had something important that the people needed to hear, and he said it. Aquila and Priscilla helped Paul at Corinth, probably started the work in Ephesus, taught Apollos, and housed the church in Rome. Luke cooperated with Paul in missionary efforts. Each was fulfilling the command of Christ, who said: "Ye shall be witnesses unto me both in Jerusalem, and in all Judaea, and in Samaria, and unto the uttermost part of the earth" (Acts 1:8).

In the world missions task there is a significant place of service for every Christian. In missions the Christian finds the most worthy investment for his life—in partnership with God, in cooperation with the Holy Spirit, in service to man, and in helping to accomplish the will of Christ.

Christian experience is incomplete without missionary outreach. This is true because Christ projected no other method for accomplishing his purpose. He did not give one commission to the individual church, another commission to the individual believer, and another commission to Christianity as a whole. There is one commission for all. The same commission applies to every church and to every believer. The command of Christ was given to all: Go! . . . make disciples . . . teach them to observe all I have commanded." This command begins with the individual as he relates to his church and his community and continues through his church to the uttermost parts of the earth.

The field is the world. Missions work takes place at home and in the "uttermost parts" simultaneously. Church members need to understand that missions is spreading the good news of salvation wherever Christ is not known, whether in another part of the city, across the nation, or across the ocean. Dr. Carver once said that missions is proclaiming the good news where it is news.

In explaining the basis of foreign missions the Foreign Mission Board gives an even more specific definition of missions and relates it to the crossing of some border (political, geographic, racial, language, cultural, or social). Carrying the gospel to other countries of the world requires crossing some obvious borders. There are also borders to cross in the United States. In fact, there are borders to cross in every community.

When a church assumes its missions responsibility in the community close at hand and on the farthest horizon, it is affirming the New Testament teachings that the missionary task is to reach from "Jerusalem and Judea" to "Samaria and to the ends of the earth." A church is constantly in need of renewing its commitment to this worldwide mission.

A church, even in its finest hours, never fully expresses Christianity, for a church is conditioned by time, by place, by circumstance, by sin. A church will devote time to revitalizing itself from within when it acknowledges the gap that exists between what it is and what Christ desires it to be. As a church links itself to the mighty purposes of God in the world, it embarks on a pilgrimage to become what it is capable of becoming under the leadership of the Holy Spirit. Only then does it know the joy of being used to fulfil a mighty purpose.

II. A CHURCH ORGANIZING TO DO ITS WORK

All churches share a common commission from Christ and to that extent they are alike, but churches differ greatly in opportunities for service. Southern Baptist churches cannot be fitted into a mold. The label "typical church" is a misnomer. Every church has distinctive and special factors which influence its work. Communities differ; members of congregations differ in background and experience; churches differ in the number of leaders and in the amount of money made available to carry on their work. For this reason, each church must decide how it will carry on the work of the Lord in the place where it is located, making the best use of its resources.

As a church studies the New Testament to discover its responsibility, it becomes concerned with being and doing what Christ intends. Then, as it understands its work, a church organizes to get the work done.

A church fulfils its responsibilities best when people are organized into working groups and responsibilities are assigned. These groups are referred to as organizations. Organization is the way people are related together to get jobs done.

Southern Baptist churches have discovered certain organizational patterns which aid them in carrying out their responsibilities. The Foreign Mission Board and Home Mission Board exist as denominational agencies, for example, to serve churches as they fulfil their missions responsibility. Church program organizations such as Woman's Missionary Union and Brotherhood are examples of working groups within a church through which the church accomplishes its missions task. Committees are other illustrations of working groups.

Organization is a means to an end, never an end in itself. Organization must be adaptable and adapted. Those who lead church program organizations must never lose sight of the purpose these organizations serve.

III. WMU—A Church Program Organization

Woman's Missionary Union is one of five church program organizations. Other church program organizations are Sunday School, Brotherhood, Training Union, and the Music Ministry. A church program organization is one which performs tasks of primary importance in helping a church accomplish its objective.

1. Tasks

Woman's Missionary Union is committed to helping a church fulfil Christ's purpose on earth. The first concern of Woman's Missionary Union, as of all church organizations, is to help a church fulfil its mission. Out of this basic concern Woman's Missionary Union finds the distinctive tasks it performs in the life and work of a church. When the work done by WMU is consistently viewed as work of the church and not just organizational work, the urgency to carry out the tasks of this organization is more compelling than ever before.

The four major tasks Woman's Missionary Union performs for a church are listed below and will be discussed in other chapters of this book:

Teach Missions
Lead persons to participate in missions
Provide organization and leadership for special missions projects of the church
Provide and interpret information regarding the work of the church and denomination.

Tasks are basic, continuing activities that must go on in the life of a church if it does its work in the world.

2. *History*

Woman's Missionary Union came into being because of the response of women to biblical teachings regarding missions and because of the sensitivity of women to missions needs which became apparent in the late eighteenth and nineteenth centuries.

When William Carey was sent out as a missionary during the latter part of the eighteenth century, the missionary urgency, which had been lost for a time, was restored. The news that Carey had left his cobbler's bench in England to go as a missionary to India set aflame the hearts of young men and women in America. Almost two decades later, in 1812, Adoniram and Ann Judson and Luther Rice left the United States for Burma. These three, who went out as Congregational missionaries, became Baptists out of conviction and were baptized in Calcutta, India, by an associate of William Carey. They were stranded, thousands of miles from home—Baptist missionaries without Baptist support. The three decided that the Judsons should move on to Burma and that Rice should return to the United States to awaken interest among Baptists and to secure financial support.

By 1813 Luther Rice was in the United States. His missionary zeal and his breadth of missionary vision were unequaled by Baptists in America at that time. He traveled to solicit support for the Judsons and to organize missionary societies. His work gave to Baptists a unity of purpose with regard to their missionary service.

In 1855 Rosewell Graves, a twenty-two-year-old doctor and son of Dr. and Mrs. John J. Graves of Baltimore, Maryland, went to China as a missionary. His going was one of the major influences which led thirty-three years later to the organization of the Southern Baptist Convention Woman's Missionary Union.

In letters Rosewell Graves urged his mother to pray for him and for the Chinese people. He suggested that she enlist other women to join her in prayer. Mrs. Graves organized the Female Missionary Prayer Meeting. For thirteen years she prayed for missions and enlisted others to pray with her.

In 1868 Mrs. Graves's opportunity came to extend the concerns of her prayer group. The Southern Baptist Convention was meeting in Baltimore, where she and her group of praying women lived. She extended an invitation to all women attending the Convention to assemble for a conference. This was the first general meeting of Southern Baptist women in the interest of missions.

Another major influence shaped the organization of Woman's Missionary Union. A young Virginia woman named Lottie Moon had gone to China in 1873 as a missionary. A magnificent idea was born in the heart of Lottie Moon which she shared through the pages of the *Foreign Mission Journal* in December, 1887:

> Some years ago the Southern Methodist Mission in China had run down to the lowest watermark; the rising of the tide seems to have begun with the enlisting of the women of the church in the cause of missions. The previously unexampled increase in missionary zeal and activity in the Northern Presbyterian church is attributed to the same reason—the thorough awakening of the women of the church upon the subject of missions. In like manner, until the women of our Southern Baptist churches are thoroughly aroused, we shall continue to go on in our present hand-to-mouth system. We shall continue to see mission stations so poorly manned that missionaries break down from overwork, loneliness, and isolation; we shall continue to see promising fields unentered and old stations languishing; and we shall continue to see other denominations no richer and no better educated than ours, outstripping us in the race. . . .
>
> I am convinced that one of the chief reasons our Southern Baptist women do so little is the lack of organization. Why should we not learn from these noble Methodist women, and instead of the paltry offering we make, do something that will prove we are really in earnest in claiming to be the followers of him who "though he was rich, for our sake became poor"? [1]

Alma Hunt says of this letter: "Thus even before formal organization took place there existed a partnership of interest and of concern between a missionary and the people at home. There was a partnership of prayer—women in the homeland praying for missionaries and missionaries praying for an awakening in the hearts of women at home which would stir them to action and organization." [2]

In 1888 in the Broad Street Methodist Church, Richmond, Virginia, Woman's Missionary Union, Auxiliary to Southern Baptist Convention was organized. The purpose of this new organization was to distribute missionary information, pray for missions, engage in missions, and give financial support to missions. This purpose of Woman's Missionary Union has remained constant through the years.

3. Age-level Organizations

Woman's Missionary Union (WMU) is made up of four age-level organizations: Woman's Missionary Society (WMS) for women above twenty-five years of age and married young women under twenty-five; Young Woman's Auxiliary (YWA) for unmarried young women, sixteen through twenty-four; Girls' Auxiliary (GA) for girls, nine through fifteen; and Sunbeam Band for boys and girls, birth through eight. Ideally, a church has as many age-level organizations as are needed to enlist the children, girls, young women, and women of the church in studying about missions and participating in missions.

IV. WMU AND MISSIONS

The Woman's Missionary Union program of a church reflects the historic purposes of WMU and grows out of five basic beliefs regarding a church and missions.

Every church has a missions responsibility.

A church's worldwide responsibility is outlined in the Bible as the work of Christ's church is set forth. A church exists to reveal Christ to the world. Southern Baptist churches have organized associations, state conventions, and the Southern Baptist Convention to assist them to do in the world what one church cannot do alone. Participation in missions by congregations and by individuals is not optional; it is an obligation assigned to all believers by Christ himself.

Since a church's responsibility beyond its immediate environment is neither easily discerned nor easily fulfilled, it seems wise for a church to organize in appropriate ways to accomplish its missions tasks. Woman's Missionary Union exists as a church program organization to help a church fulfil its missions responsibility.

A church's missions responsibility includes teaching missions, praying for missions, giving for the support of missions, and witnessing and ministering through mission action.

Women's groups responded first to world need by praying for missions and giving to support missions. Soon the formal study of missions was added to provide understanding and to motivate persons to pray and to give. Later in Woman's Missionary Union history the dimension of personal service was added to make missions concern intensely practical in the community served by the church.

The assumption which underlies these missionary activities is the belief that knowing God's teachings about his purpose results in a logical and proper expression of this purpose in the life of each Christian. Living out the implications of Christ's statement, "As my Father hath sent me, even so send I you" (John 20:21), becomes the major objective of a Christian's life on earth.

Witnessing is imperative because the redemption of lost persons is at stake. A Christian who has the compassion of Christ cannot neglect this. Ministering is necessary because Christians have a responsibility to meet the basic human needs of persons in the name of Jesus Christ. Followers of Christ are challenged daily with finding ways to meet these needs. Praying is vital, for it is the means, from the human standpoint, for effecting the growth of the kingdom on earth and for knowing and doing God's will. Through intercessory prayer a Christian can witness and minister to the ends of the earth. Giving for the support of missions is significant because it is an act of worship. To the degree that Christians recognize that they belong to Christ, they will give of material wealth to support his work everywhere.

If the task of world missions is to be carried out, each Christian must determine before God his degree of dedication to the task.

The study of missions and other actions are specialized parts of the total church program.

Many of the educational efforts of a Southern Baptist church are expended to sustain the church, to reach people for church membership, and to cultivate the life of the church and its constituents. The specialized study of missions in Woman's Missionary Union alerts church members to awareness and response to the mission of the church beyond its immediate witness—to the end of the world. Missionary education reaches into the reservoir of information and concepts about a church's total mission and brings into focus a church's mission beyond sustaining itself.

Mission action, or community missions, is the capstone of missionary education. Through the years the practical expression of missionary concern has been vital to Woman's Missionary Union. At the performance stage of their work, Southern Baptist churches expend much of their resources meeting needs of their constituency and reaching prospects for church membership; but a church's mission in its environment must take into account the total needs of all people. Many persons who will require specialized ministries will never become members of the church attempting to meet these needs. This is a ministry without any thought of gain for a church. Study experiences in Woman's Missionary Union provide information for members which helps motivate them to engage in this type of ministry. Women have been diligent in mission action in response to the challenge of the needs of people in their church community.

A woman's organization can perform specialized missions tasks in behalf of the church.

The Bible speaks clearly regarding the missionary responsibility of every Christian and of the attentive services rendered by women. Mary Magdalene's ministry to Jesus, the women's watch at the tomb, and the activities of women in the early church are examples from the Bible of woman's response to need. Women have been key figures in the beginnings and growth of mission societies among Baptists. This is a modern example of woman's response to opportunity and need.

By nature women are sensitive to human need. This innate sensitivity, endowed by God, has caused women to respond in self-giving ministries to meet the needs of persons in Jesus' name. Women's spontaneous response to prayer requests from missions fields verifies the fact that women are sensitive to missions needs.

By nature women are creative. A woman's function in society requires that she cultivate her creative instincts. Christian women are challenged by the creative demands of missions. Early in the history of WMU there are evidences that women were imaginative in their responses to missions needs as they designed channels of response. Southern Baptists have wisely capitalized on the innate creativity of women by giving them responsibility to help fulfil the missions concerns of the denomination.

By nature women are helpers. In the design of God this role is natural and right. In a church, WMU is one of five program organizations through which a church does its work. Women can easily grasp and implement the concept of a church organization "helping the church fulfil its mission."

Courts Redford, former executive secretary of the Home

Mission Board, said of woman's contribution to missions:

> Wherever she is, a woman will be molding the life of her community and shaping the destiny of the world.
>
> In thus serving mankind the Christian woman will likely choose the church as a channel through which her love may flow. That love enriches her own life, blesses her children, stabilizes her home, helps her community and reaches out through her prayers and gifts to minister to the whole world.
>
> This woman will likely use mission agencies in extending her love and her influence. Her love is expressed and exemplified in prayer and concern for the unreached multitudes and the faithful missionaries. Her zeal is manifest in loving service where consecrated feet may tread and faithful hands may serve.
>
> She will extend that compassion and ministry to faraway areas and to persons behind language and social barriers. Through her love gifts she will multiply her ministries all across the land.
>
> By studying the needs and opportunities for specialized ministries and the best channels through which they may be supported, she will enrich her ministries.
>
> Women's love will light the fires of evangelistic zeal and missionary fervor that will supply adequate support and lead scores to place their lives on the altar for mission service.
>
> Such is the triumph and victory of a woman's love.[3]

The total church must be involved in missions.

The Bible makes clear the world mission of a church and the individual member's responsibility in a church's total work. Missions is a part of this work. Historically, the program of missionary education in a Southern Baptist church has been conducted by a woman's organization for women, young women, girls, and children. At the same time, WMU has conducted projects which made possible missions involvement beyond WMU membership. Examples are the weeks of prayer for foreign and home missions, the Lottie Moon Christmas Offering, the Annie Armstrong Offering, and the study of missions books.

In these ways, Woman's Missionary Union extends to all church members opportunities for study, guided prayer, giving, and mission action. In doing this, Woman's Missionary Union coordinates its efforts with Brotherhood—the missionary organization for men, young men, and boys—to reach the entire church membership with a continuing program of study and action.

Changing the world for Christ can happen only as each church takes seriously its mission, only as each organization of a church marshals its full resources to do the work of a church, and only as each church member becomes seriously concerned about knowing and doing God's will.

A pastor, contemplating his responsibility for missions, wrote these words:

> "I am a pastor. There are some musts for me.
>   I must keep missions alive in my heart
>   I must learn missions
>   I must help call out missionaries
>   I must preach missions
>   I must teach missions
>   I must lead the church to give to missions
>   I must put missions first
>   I must know the missions field
>   I must lead the people of my church to
>   be missionaries in spirit." [4]

To this pastor, and to others who share his concern, Woman's Missionary Union exists as a helper, assuming a share of the load, participating in the burden of concern, and working to help a church fulfil in the largest sense its reason for being.

CHAPTER 2

I. Importance of Teaching Missions

II. Church Members as Learners

III. Content for Teaching Missions
  1. Missionary Message of the Bible
  2. Progress of Christian Missions
  3. Contemporary Missions Work of Southern Baptists

IV. Relationships in Teaching Missions
  1. Woman's Missionary Union and Brotherhood
  2. Woman's Missionary Union and Sunday School
  3. Woman's Missionary Union and Training Union
  4. Woman's Missionary Union and Music Ministry

2

Teaching Missions

CHRIST'S INVITATION to those who would follow him was: "Take my yoke upon you, and learn of me; for I am meek and lowly in heart: and ye shall find rest unto your souls" (Matt. 11:29). Every Christian should be a learner; every church has a teaching function. The commission of Christ clearly embodies the command "teaching them to observe all things." Teaching is central in the purpose of the church, for Christian growth is dependent upon learning.

A teaching church will provide a well-rounded educational program for its members. This will include studies in many areas of content, such as the biblical revelation, Christian ethics, Christian history, systematic theology, church polity and organization, music, and missions. Study in all these areas by church members establishes them in the Christian faith and prepares them to express their faith daily.

Teaching missions is a vital and significant part of the church's total educational program. This distinctive task is shared by Woman's Missionary Union and Brotherhood, the missions organizations in a church. Studying missions keeps church members aware that they have responsibility not only for the people in the community served by the church but also for people of the world.

Church members will never be deeply involved in missions apart from a regular program of missionary education. Woman's Missionary Union assists the church by providing opportunities for a specialized and an intensive study of missions.

In teaching missions, Woman's Missionary Union leads church members to explore with growing understanding the nature and implications of God's missionary purpose and to respond to that purpose in personal commitment and obedience. Awareness and response to God's missionary purpose is a lifelong task for Christians. This learning task has meaning for the youngest child engaged in study as well as for the mature adult who is still growing in an understanding of the Christian faith and life.

Throughout the life span, church members need to explore the truth about God's missionary purpose as set forth in the Bible. They need to discover ways churches fulfil God's missionary purpose, both in the historical and in the contemporary setting. Church members must prayerfully consider the meaning of God's missionary purpose in today's world. Then, these understandings reached under the leadership of the Holy Spirit must be applied in personal experience as each person assumes responsibility for missions.

I. Importance of Teaching Missions

The study of missions is one of the most challenging of all educational opportunities in the church. This study holds a strategic place of importance because it helps keep a church aware of and responsive to its missions task. For this reason, each church should plan for missionary education to be offered to all members. The programs of Woman's Missionary Union and Brotherhood in a church potentially can offer missionary education to all church members.

The study of missions can help a church achieve its reason for being. A growing understanding of God's redemptive plan keeps a church aware of the universality of its mission and the scope of its responsibility.

The study of missions encourages church members to assume their responsibility in the contemporary world. While the message of redemption is unchanging, the world in which the message is told is constantly changing. Church members must understand both the message and the contemporary world if they are to comprehend and accept their missionary task.

The study of missions cultivates concern in the home, the community, the nation, and the world. In most instances church members who are shortsighted and self-centered in their concern are those who are not informed about the needs of lost persons around the world.

The study of missions helps motivate Christians to invest their lives and resources in missions. Knowledge of the need for missionaries will challenge young people to consider investing their lives in vocational missionary service. The same information will challenge church members to accept the missionary implication of their Christian calling, whatever their daily work may be. Appeals for financial and prayer support for missions are more effective when persons understand their relationship to the world missions task of Christ. A large number of churches have not given their members a basic understanding of the stewardship of life out of which generous offerings come. Many Southern Baptists are still confined in thought and action to their own neighborhood. And some are often more concerned with themselves than with the needs of the multitudes of lost persons around the world. If these observations are true, it is because there has not been sufficient information to challenge and motivate church members. The studies in Woman's Missionary Union cause church members to lift up their eyes upon the fields and to respond to the needs they see.

Woman's Missionary Union recognizes the close relationship which should exist between the educational activities of the church and the educational activities in a Christian home. In teaching missions, this relationship is especially important.

Mrs. William McMurry in her book *Educating Youth in Missions* expressed well the concern of Woman's Missionary Union. She said: "Woman's Missionary Union believes and teaches that missionary education should begin in the home. No one can estimate the influence that parents have exerted in arousing and developing right attitudes in missionary interest on the part of their children. Little children absorb the negative feelings of their mothers in particular. The flash of an eye, a shrug of the shoulder, the tone of the voice, a spirit of indifference are caught long before a child can understand the words. The reverse is also true. What children hear their parents say about the preacher, the church, giving of money, missions, and missionaries colors their thinking all through life. The deposit, whether negative or positive, has been made in their minds and hearts and will remain." [1]

II. CHURCH MEMBERS AS LEARNERS

The teaching of missions assumes that there are students to be taught. A church teaches through its leaders and its curriculum; church members and members of church organizations are the learners. Teaching and learning are reverse sides of the same coin. Learning in the Christian context is designed to bring about changes in persons in their relationship to God and in their relationship to other persons. Teaching, on the other hand, is planning for and guiding the learning experiences which will bring about these desired changes. Education is the term which describes the teaching-learning process.

Woman's Missionary Union is concerned with the teacher and the learner. Beginning with the youngest child in Sunbeam Band and continuing with the mature adult in Woman's Missionary Society, Woman's Missionary Union guides its members as they grow in their understanding of and response to missions. Maturing in missions concepts implies change. Change occurs primarily in the learner's knowledge, understandings, appreciations, attitudes, and skills as they relate to missions.

Knowledge covers the subject matter or basic information mastered by the learner. Understandings are the meanings the learner perceives from the subject matter studied. Appreciations are the values or worth placed on that which is learned. Attitudes are the learner's feelings and response to what is being learned. Skills involve the ability to use one's knowledge effectively.

No church member would boast that he knows as much as he needs to know about the world in which he lives and God's purpose in that world. Because of inadequate information, there is a lack of understanding of the people of the world, the circumstances under which they live, and the means by which they are being reached with the gospel. The cycle continues. Because of a lack of understanding or lack of appreciation, a church member sometimes holds attitudes toward the missions task and toward people of the world which are not conducive to effective missions concern. Woman's Missionary Union, through a sustained program of mission study, seeks to change this. Woman's Missionary Union seeks to develop a growing understanding of God's missionary purpose, an understanding of the people of the world, and a knowledge of the missions work being carried on by missionaries around the world. With this knowledge and understanding comes growth in compassion and concern for sharing the gospel with the whole world.

Learning takes place best when a person recognizes his need to learn. When this happens the goal of learning becomes personal and a person puts forth energy and effort to achieve it. A great educator once said, "The best time to learn something is when one feels acutely uncomfortable about not knowing it."

In Christian education the Holy Spirit intervenes in the

learning process. Paul told the Galatians: "For neither did I receive it from a human being nor was I taught it, except through revelation of Jesus Christ" (Gal. 1:12, Berkeley).

The Holy Spirit in his nearness and presence helps a Christian know himself, God, and God's will for him. The Holy Spirit awakens, guides, and enables him to think, feel, choose, and live as he ought. He instructs a Christian in all truth.

The capacity to learn is God-given. God is active in a person's processes of learning. The Holy Spirit is active in the learner, calling him to become all he is capable of becoming as a child of God.

When a person learns, it is natural that he begins to act in response to what he has learned. When the first-grader rushes home to read, "Oh, oh, oh, Look, look, look," he is demonstrating a basic fact about learning: Learning is intended to result in action.

The teaching of missions in churches began with the modern missionary movement. As societies for the support of missions began to spring up in the latter part of the eighteenth century, there was a growing recognition that prayer for missions and the financial support of missions must be undergirded by adequate information about missions. This led to the study of missions in an intensive way. The recognition existed then, as it does today, that what a person ultimately does in behalf of missions springs from adequate information, proper understanding, deepened appreciations, improved attitudes, and developed skills.

III. CONTENT FOR TEACHING MISSIONS

To develop understanding of the full scope of missions, Woman's Missionary Union leads church members to study the missionary message of the Bible, the progress of Christian missions, and the contemporary missions work of Southern Baptists. Viewing missions from these three vantage points builds an understanding of the nature and implications of God's missionary purpose in the world.

1. *Missionary Message of the Bible*

To be called missionary, a church must lead its members to develop an understanding of missions based on biblical concepts. This understanding results from a study of the missionary message of the Bible.

J. B. Lawrence, who served as the executive secretary of the Home Mission Board, said: "There are two ways by which missionary zeal is created and maintained: one, the study of missionary facts; the other, the study of the Bible as a missionary book. These two methods should be combined for the best results." [2]

Mrs. McMurry said: "The great theme of the Bible is missionary in character. God's plan for worldwide redemption is the heart of his written Word. Without a knowledge of the Bible's primary message there can be no deeply anchored motive for the modern-day proclamation of the gospel. . . . The Bible is essentially a missionary book." [3]

This interpretation of the Bible is WMU's basis for teaching church members the biblical concept of missions. God's redeeming activity, the heart of missions, is apparent throughout the Old Testament. He created the universe and everything in it, and he loved his creation. When men alienated themselves from him, he forgave and redeemed them in his love. He chastised them and instructed them so that they might know him and live in fellowship with him. Ultimately he called Israel to be his chosen and holy people that they might become his witnesses to the nations.

There are many specific Old Testament teachings regarding missions. God commanded Moses to tell the Israelites to make God known to their children and to their children's children. Jonah went to Nineveh to witness. Ezekiel knew that the righteous should warn the unrighteous. The prophets declared God's purpose. The psalmist taught others to declare God's truths.

God's purpose and desire have always been that all men everywhere should be redeemed. The New Testament records God's redeeming love and reconciling act in Jesus Christ and outlines in bold strokes a church's responsibility for missions. The missionary imperative is written in large letters over the entire New Testament.

When Christ came into the world, he began the missionary enterprise. He became the mediator of God's love to man, bringing sinful man back to a right relationship with God the Father. Christ organized and explained God's missionary plan. After his resurrection, Jesus explained to the disciples that it would be best for them if he were to leave them. While on earth he could be in only one place, but after his ascension he would send the Holy Spirit, who could be with all believers in all places at all times.

The New Testament sets forth the work of the Holy Spirit in directing and inspiring God's missionary plan. The coming of the Holy Spirit at Pentecost is an important day in the history of missions because it marks the beginning of a group effort to win others to Christ. Christ's command to the disciples to wait for the Holy Spirit was equally as important as his command to go. Today the Holy Spirit is continuing the work of Christ on earth, stimulating spiritual growth, working within the unbeliever's heart to convict him of sin, and calling individual Christians into missionary service.

Participation in missions is inherent in discipleship. Participation in missions is also the natural expression of the church, the body of Christ. God's purpose in Christ was redemption. The sharing of the good news about redemption is the stewardship of the church; therefore, the church, collectively and individually, is committed to missions.

In the New Testament, Jesus' teachings and examples

make it clear that every Christian is a witness. Jesus made every encounter an opportunity to lead persons to faith in himself.

The response at Pentecost, the scattering of Christians because of persecution, and the spirit and zeal of Paul are a few of the New Testament examples which show that the early Christians felt the compulsion to proclaim their faith.

After his death and resurrection, Jesus climaxed his teachings by saying: "Go ye." This command was without reference to territory. Christians are to be witnesses to the uttermost part of the earth and are to make disciples of all nations.

Any understanding of missions must be based on the biblical concepts of missions as contained in the Bible—God's missionary book. Woman's Missionary Union teaches these concepts.

2. *Progress of Christian Missions*

When the Jerusalem Christians were scattered because of persecution, "they went everywhere preaching the word." Churches were motivated to witness. In the course of daily contacts, Christians carried the gospel message wherever their travels and trade took them. Because of this, little groups of believers were formed in many lands. This method of missionary expansion was one of the secrets of the remarkable spread of early Christianity, despite persecution.

In the Middle Ages the church became more highly institutionalized. Churches grew larger and more influential, and the tendency to emphasize the church as an institution increased. During this time, evangelization and missionary efforts became official and corporate rather than spontaneous and individual.

During the Reformation, churches made limited response to their missionary responsibility. This period made little contribution to evangelical missions except for the migration of Christians to North America. The reformers held that the missionary responsibility of the church ended with the apostles, since it was to them that the original commission had been given.

By the end of the eighteenth century, however, interest in missions had begun to increase among Protestants. Although this interest had not yet become churchwide, groups of individual Christians began to organize themselves into missionary societies for the support of missions. William Carey was sent by the London Missionary Society as its missionary to India. His going, in 1793, marked the beginning of the modern missionary movement. Interested people began to join themselves together into societies to encourage and to support missionaries. These organizations grew in number, both in Europe and in America. Gradually denominations began to accept missions as an important sphere of activity.

In 1845, when the Southern Baptist Convention was formed, one of its first acts was to establish the Board of Domestic Missions and the Foreign Mission Board. Then, in 1888 the organization of Woman's Missionary Union added impetus to the missions cause. Gaines S. Dobbins said that the organization of Woman's Missionary Union brought missions into the churches with intelligent ardor matched by prayer and sacrificial giving and put the missionary cause into the mainstream of the life of the churches.

A study of the progress of Christian missions is a study of the advance which has been made in carrying out Christ's commission. Christians should know the conditions and circumstances under which the gospel has progressed from the ascension of Christ to the present so they can relate themselves effectively to the never-ending missionary task. Christians need to know how present-day missionary efforts are hampered or helped by what has happened in history.

A striking example of the influence of history on contemporary missions work can be found in the Middle East. The Foreign Mission Board secretary for Europe and the Middle East said in one of his reports that resistance to Christianity in the Middle East cannot be understood without a knowledge of what the crusades (military expeditions undertaken by Christians in the eleventh, twelfth, and thirteenth centuries to recover the Holy Land from the Muslims) have done to the minds of the people. This part of the world seems to present a cold shoulder and a deaf ear to what people say in words. They remember the crusader with his sword and his spear and his shield. These people are looking to what Christians do, not just to what they say.

Woman's Missionary Union guides persons in acquiring a general knowledge of missions history and in developing a more specific understanding of the history of missions in various countries of the world.

3. Contemporary Missions Work of Southern Baptists

A thorough study of the current situation in missions must have full consideration by church members. People live in the here and now. The situation in missions today must be understood for individuals to know how to relate to missions.

A major portion of the study time in WMU organizations is given to learning about contemporary missions. This study leads to an understanding of the missions work carried on by the Home and Foreign Mission Boards of the Southern Baptist Convention. It provides background information about the broad geographical and sociological areas where Southern Baptists have missions work and creates an appreciation for the factors which influence the types of missions work carried on in these areas. The study explains how missions work is done and builds understanding of trends in missions. It offers ways in which each church member may become involved in missions where he is and presents various opportunities for actual missionary service.

An understanding of the basic beliefs regarding missions and missionary work is essential to understanding the missions program of Southern Baptists. This study is based on the redemptive plan of God and the role of the Christian as an instrument of redemption. It includes a discussion of ways to witness to persons under the influence of different cultures, religions, value systems, and philosophies of life. The study also deals with the various methods and techniques of Christian missions. Some Christian groups expend their resources on direct evangelism, while others have developed extensive medical and educational ministries. A study of various approaches to missions work helps Southern Baptists to become aware of all possible means of communicating the gospel of Christ to the people of the world.

The study of other religions is also a part of the study of contemporary missions, for what these groups believe helps determine the methods used by Southern Baptist missionaries who work among them. In addition to Christianity, there are ten major religions in the world today. Each of these religions has its own distinctive cultural setting and historical development which influence missions methods.

The study of the contemporary work done by churches through the Home and Foreign Mission Boards receives major attention in the WMU curriculum. The work of the Foreign Mission Board is conducted in areas beyond the United States. The Home Mission Board, primarily through cooperative agreements with state conventions, is responsible for developing a plan for missions work in the United States. The varied missions approaches of these boards demonstrate versatility in meeting human needs and in bringing men to God.

In the book *Woman's Missionary Union,* Alma Hunt points up the basic relationship of Woman's Missionary Union to the mission boards of the Southern Baptist Convention. Two of the significant areas of relationship with these boards are as follows: "Informing Southern Baptist women and young people about the needs of the people of the world for the gospel and the efforts of the two mission boards to meet these needs . . . and preparing . . . youth for God's call as missionaries and for their future support by those not so called." [4]

The study of types, philosophy, and techniques of Southern Baptist missions work is incomplete without knowledge of the resources which make the work possible. The resources are prayer, finances, and missionary personnel. Biblical and historical sources emphasize the place of prayer in the work of missions. The study of needs for missionary personnel deals with the biblical teachings concerning the missionary implications of the Christian calling. This study further teaches the philosophy and procedure used by mission boards in sending out and supporting missionaries. The content for the study of the financial support of missions work includes the principles of stewardship of possessions and the media for supporting missions. These media are the church budget, the Cooperative Program, and missions offerings.

A study of Southern Baptist resources takes into account the opportunities for training for missionary responsibility. Units of study in WMU emphasize the place and importance of churches, homes, colleges, universities, and theological seminaries in missionary education.

Woman's Missionary Union also provides study opportunities which inform church members of world conditions and trends affecting missions. These conditions and trends include economic, technological, spiritual, and sociocultural forces which create the environment in which missions work is undertaken. On the national level, these same forces are at work. No two sections of the United States are alike. Sections of the country differ in political alignment, economic levels, social classes, educational levels, and religious orientation. These and other environmental factors are studied in WMU as a background for understanding Southern Baptist missions.

An awareness of the contemporary world and the missions work being done in the world is essential in involving churches in the missions endeavor. Awareness is "seeing with the mind and heart." It adds special dimension to life, allowing Christians not only to look, but also to see; not only to listen, but also to hear. Awareness stabs the heart in bringing concern, possesses the emotions in developing compassion, penetrates the mind in deepening understanding, and displaces attitudes which form barriers to involvement in missions.

IV. RELATIONSHIPS IN TEACHING MISSIONS

The study of missions in WMU is one part of the total curriculum of Southern Baptist churches. Woman's Missionary Union and Brotherhood serve the church by teaching missions. Other content areas are studied in other church program organizations. Because the study of missions in WMU is one part of a whole curriculum in a church, there are significant relationships between WMU and other church organizations. The following list shows church program organizations and the content areas which are dealt with by each one:

Organization	*Content Areas*
Sunday School	Biblical Revelation
Brotherhood	Missions
Woman's Missionary Union	Missions
Training Union	Systematic Theology
	Christian History
	Christian Ethics
	Church Polity and Organization
Music Ministry	Music and Hymnody

Being aware of the teaching responsibility of each church program organization makes understanding relationships easier. Each organization has a teaching task, but the content to be taught by each is distinctive. Together, these organizations offer balanced and comprehensive study opportunities to members of a church.

1. *Woman's Missionary Union and Brotherhood*

A vital relationship exists between Woman's Missionary Union and Brotherhood in teaching missions in a church. These two organizations share the task: Teach missions. The content to be taught by each organization is the same, but the membership of each is different. Together, these organizations have the potential for reaching the entire church membership with missionary education and information.

2. *Woman's Missionary Union and Sunday School*

In teaching missions, Woman's Missionary Union has a relationship to what is taught in Sunday School. The Sunday School, in teaching the biblical revelation, leads persons in a study of God's disclosure of himself and his will for man as recorded in the Bible. Such a study provides the basis for Christian missions. The Bible is the record and interpretation of God's deeds in history and of the experiences of his people in relationship to these deeds. The more profound one's knowledge of biblical revelation becomes, the clearer one's sense of missionary responsibility becomes. The study of missions begins with the Bible. Woman's Missionary Union leads persons into a specialized study of the missionary message of the Bible, which traces the thread of missions in God's unfolding revelation.

In the study of the biblical revelation in Sunday School, missions will emerge naturally as one of the themes; but in the study of missions in Woman's Missionary Union, the study will major on the missions theme, exploring the depth of its meaning and interpreting the implications of its message.

3. Woman's Missionary Union and Training Union

The study in Woman's Missionary Union also relates to studies which take place in Training Union. This relationship is seen most clearly when each of the content areas of Training Union is looked at separately.

The study of missions is closely related to the study of Christian history in Training Union. From history one learns how far churches have progressed in carrying out the Great Commission. While the study of Christian history in Training Union gives the broad historical base of Christianity, the study of missions deals with the missions aspect of this history as a basis for understanding the plans and methods of contemporary missions.

The "why" of missions is learned from systematic theology. A study of systematic theology encourages persons to look critically at their beliefs and to reaffirm them in light of the Scriptures. The foundations of Christian missions are rooted in the character and purpose of God, the nature and needs of man, and other basic doctrinal concepts which are within the scope of systematic theology.

The study of church polity and organization in Training Union brings understanding of the ways people are related together to get jobs done in the church and in the denomination. This study provides a background for understanding the way Baptists have organized to carry out the Great Commission.

The study of Christian ethics in Training Union develops an understanding of what is right conduct in light of God's character. It is the study of the application of the gospel in the whole field of man's relationships. Christian missions and man's response to others influence his witness, regardless of the distance. The same is true of a group of Christians whether this group is a congregation or a denomination. Some of the greatest problems facing missions today exist because Christians have failed to apply the teachings of Christ in all areas of life. An honest study of ethics undergirds and adds dimension to the study of missions. The application of Christian ethics to life situations helps create a climate in which the Christian gospel can be proclaimed most effectively. The study of ethics cultivates insights that operate in the Christian's treatment of his fellowmen, at home or abroad. WMU builds on these understandings, both in the study of missions and in the participation of members in local missions work.

4. *Woman's Missionary Union and Music Ministry*

Woman's Missionary Union also relates to the content area taught by the Music Ministry. Christianity is a singing religion. The imperative for missions has been stated in many hymns of the Christian faith. Music can help motivate persons to awareness and response to world missions. Music also contributes to more effective worship in the church, which strengthens a church for realizing its mission in the world.

The study of missions in Woman's Missionary Union brings together into a meaningful whole the missions content which emerges in the studies of other organizations plus contemporary missions. Bringing content together in this way allows for concentrated depth study. A depth study of missions is significant in the life of a church. The major resources of other church program organizations are spent in helping a church realize its mission in its immediate area— reaching people for church membership and cultivating the life of a church itself and of its constituents. In contrast, the study of missions in Woman's Missionary Union and

Brotherhood is leading a church to awareness and response to its mission beyond its immediate witness.

When the studies offered by each church organization are brought together, they form a comprehensive curriculum for the church. This total curriculum provides church members with a well-rounded educational experience, which forms the base for Christian service.

CHAPTER 3

I. A Church Responds to the World

II. Personal Involvement in Missions

III. Areas of Participation in Missions
    1. Praying for Missions
    2. Giving for the Support of Missions
    3. Witnessing and Ministering Through Mission Action

IV. Relationships in Participation in Missions
    1. Woman's Missionary Union and Brotherhood
    2. Woman's Missionary Union and Sunday School
    3. Woman's Missionary Union and Training Union
    4. Woman's Missionary Union and the Missions Committee

3

Leading Participation in Missions

STUDY ABOUT MISSIONS should result in participation in missions.

Study without response can be like the woman who decided to write a book. She added a room to her house and filled shelves in it with resource books. She bought a desk, a new typewriter, paper, carbon paper, and eraser; sharpened her pencils, and then rocked in her new desk chair.

Learning and doing are bound together. Study about missions should lead to involvement in missions. Many church members are actively involved in opportunities for learning and are inactive in doing the work of a church. Williams' translation of Matthew 28:20 expresses this idea of participation: "Teach them to practice all the commands that I have given you."

One pastor expressed his concern this way: "I have attended many meetings at the church which thrilled my heart, but the thrill soon left as I realized that the persons in those meetings were talking about Christianity and about missions, but they were not living their Christian faith and practicing what they professed to believe. How can this be changed?"

This question posed by a pastor nags at every sensitive church leader who lives with the realization that a margin exists between what some Christians profess to be and what they are. One way to get at the answer to this question is to establish a more vital relationship between study and other actions.

The WMU task of leading persons to participate in missions recognizes that study about missions should lead ultimately to action. Participation implies being involved in the missionary enterprise. To participate in missions is to be individually involved in the process of world redemption, both in the presentation of the saving gospel of Jesus Christ and the alleviation of human need in Christ's name.

I. A Church Responds to the World

Christians as individuals and collectively as churches are confronted daily by the needs of every man.

> I saw need today.
> It wore so many faces
> And when it was unmasked
> It was Every Man.
>
> I saw
> pain without healing
> hunger gaping from hollow sockets
> the spectral stare of blindness
> sorrow looking through a tear-woven veil.
>
> I shrank from what I saw.[1]

A yawning gap exists between those who have and those who have not. Christians realize that awareness of need demands response, but what are they to do? What can be done for the people in the world who do not know what it is to be well fed or for those who have never heard the name of Jesus? The world—with its blind and its deaf; its poor and its slum dwellers; its artists, musicians, and poets; its sick; its affluent urban families; its rebels; its seekers—is the responsibility of every Christian because every Christian belongs to Christ and is a colaborer of his (1 Cor. 3).

Jesus had something personal to say about how a Christian should respond to need. To some he said: Sell all you have; share your possessions with the poor; and come, follow me. To those who heard him tell the story of the good Samaritan he said, "You go and practice that same way!" (Luke 10:37, Berkeley).

Zacchaeus' response to Jesus' request was courageous. He was willing to restore fourfold. The average Southern Baptist may not feel that he has wronged anyone to the degree that Zacchaeus had; but as long as his closet is full of clothes and his cabinet is full of food, every Christian needs to consider what he can share.

Mary responded by pouring all her ointment on Jesus' feet. She did not say: "Take this. I don't need it anyway." She exhibited to Christians this truth: The closer one is to Jesus the more compelled he is to pour out his best.

God's eternal purpose in Christ is redemption for all men through the grace of God. The stewardship of this grace is committed to Christians. Meeting physical and spiritual needs of persons is central for a Christian. As he participates in missions, a Christian can, in a small way, show gratitude for God's act of mercy in saving him. God's design for the redemption of all persons is that believers will tell others. Every believer is meant to be a witness.

Participation in missions is central for a Christian and is essential for a church. The church is the body of Christ, and Christ projects himself in the world through the church. Because this is true, all the realities of the Christian experience come to focus in the word mission. As a church worships, learns, witnesses, and ministers, it is not exercising an option; it is expressing in the fullest sense its reason for being.

Early Christians "went forth and preached everywhere." When asked why, they had but one answer: The love of Christ constrains them. To the degree that a present-day Christian yields himself to this love, he finds himself desiring above all else to express this love by sharing the news of salvation with others.

A Christian gives himself to missions to the degree that he has compassion for a lost world. Compassion comes through an understanding of the plight of those who are lost without God. The more a church member knows about human misery, the more insight he has into the hopelessness of unbelief. Everything a Christian has which is most meaningful to him, a lost person lacks: eternal life, the fellowship of other Christians, Christmas, Easter, hymns to sing, prayer opportunities, the opportunity to be an instrument of God through which his salvation may reach others.

II. Personal Involvement in Missions

While the church is the enterprise through which missions work is done, the unit of service in this enterprise is the individual Christian. Every person has the potential for participation in world missions, whether the place is on a home or foreign missions field or in the community. The Great Commission places emphasis on making disciples.

Ever-enlarging opportunities for participation in world missions confront the Christian. Technological advances in transportation and communication and a mobile population have combined to plant thousands of Southern Baptists in the middle of missions fields overseas and in the United States. As Baptist churches live up to their responsibilities, they provide not only money and prayer support for missions but also nonprofessional missionaries who are employed by private or government agencies overseas and nonprofessional missionaries and evangelists in the United States. The persons who bear individual and continuous witness to their faith support and reinforce missions efforts overseas and in difficult areas in the United States.

Communism, nationalism, and Islam have been making vast strides toward world domination by means of nonprofessional witnesses. The Christian church, in her most expansive age, did the same. In the twentieth century there are frontiers of involvement to be explored and courageously entered by individuals.

There are frontiers of personal involvement in missions which can be expressed by persons who stay at home. Helen Fling in *Enlistment for Missions* wrote of woman's role in missions: "Today's woman may live in a cozy little house on a quiet little street, but no longer can she live in a cozy little world unto herself. . . . This is a world without walls. A sincere Christian woman can never be a spiritual isolationist. Having declared her faith in One who became involved in the world for man's salvation, she too must become involved in the cause for which Christ died." [2]

Participation in missions involves attitudes, opinions, and convictions expressed in the home and community. In these times of controversial social issues and international tensions, what a Christian thinks and how he expresses his thoughts are important. Attitudes of forgiveness, generosity, compassion, peace, and world-mindedness support Christian missions. Bigotry, prejudice, pride, and indifference undermine missions.

The attitudes of Christians and of churches toward other races affect world missions. Interracial conflicts literally cut off the channels of witnessing to the people of other colors all over the world. Missionaries find it difficult to equate gifts and attitudes when gifts seem to reflect generous hearts and attitudes seem to reflect limited willingness to share the gospel.

When a person is committed to missions, the spirit of missions will influence his attitude in all associations in life— home, profession, civic and social activities. This person will be an ardent and intelligent supporter of missions. He will have keen sensitivity to the need for praying, giving money, and sharing his abilities to strengthen the Christian witness in every part of the earth.

"Leading persons to participate in missions" is a church

task. As Woman's Missionary Union gives leadership to this task in a church, this organization recognizes a responsibility beyond its membership to involve all women, young women, girls, and children of the church in missions. The Brotherhood reaches men, young men, and boys.

To "lead persons" means to guide or direct in action. Such guidance is an organization responsibility. "Leading" means relating persons to a learning environment or atmosphere which motivates the expression of missionary concern in action, and it means planning and conducting activities in which persons can participate.

Participation in missions should be both spontaneous and planned. Mission action may be engaged in both by individuals and by groups. While the individual has many opportunities for witness and ministry, growing out of his spontaneous response to the needs of people, he must also see his responsibilities which can best be expressed as he relates to others in planned group activities. The family group is rich in its potential for mission action. Likewise, groups of individuals within the corporate body of the church can be related together to engage in missions activities.

The impulse to be personally involved in missions was the motivating force which brought WMU organizations into being. Scattered groups of women, sensing the needs of missionaries, met to pray for them and to give money for their support. Later the formalized study of missions was added to undergird the actions of praying and giving. In 1909, twenty-one years after the organization of Woman's Missionary Union, the work of "personal service" was added to the WMU program. Later, this concept was enlarged and called community missions. Thus, through the years, WMU has engaged in a significant program of missionary service in the community. This action phase was in addition to praying for and giving to missions.

All members of a church need to know how they can relate

their lives and resources to missions. Where the individual can go, he becomes a missionary. Where the individual cannot go, he becomes involved in missions through his resources. This philosophy of involvement in missions guides Woman's Missionary Union in carrying out the task: Lead persons to participate in missions.

Personal involvement refers to the act of engaging Southern Baptists absorbingly and engrossingly in the work of missions. It implies using self—time, ability, money, influence, witness—in missionary work. Involving Baptists means moving missions from the edge of their concern to the center. It means making missions central for every Christian so that he acts spontaneously and personally in response to world need and participates in the missions program and projects planned by his church.

The late Mrs. William McMurry, who devoted her life to a study of missions and influencing others to join in this study, pointed out that Confucius gave his people one corner of an idea, expecting them to find the other three. Awareness of world needs is one corner of the basic purpose of Woman's Missionary Union. Once church members have felt the crushing weight of the lostness of mankind and the needs of the world, they will find the remaining corners of the missionary idea: praying for missions, giving for the support of missions, and witnessing and ministering through mission action. Mrs. McMurry said on many occasions: "It is not enough to pray, 'God, make me aware,' but add 'God, make me a participant.'"

III. AREAS OF PARTICIPATION IN MISSIONS

The followers of Christ are to be participants with him in a world task. Missions is conquest. Permeation of the world with the gospel is inherent in the very nature of Christianity. World conquest in behalf of Christ demands active participation by Christians.

Woman's Missionary Union has helped create an environment in churches in which persons can hear and respond to the call of God to vocational missionary service. This is one way to participate in missions.

Mrs. Freddie Joe Snyder, serving as a missionary in Lebanon, says: "My interest in foreign missions had its beginning the year I was YWA president at First Baptist Church, Borger, Texas. I frequently recall our theme song:

> O Zion, haste, thy mission, high fulfilling,
> To tell to all the world that God is light;
> That He who made all nations is not willing
> One soul should perish, lost in shades of night.

These words have emphatically remained a message to my life."

A missionary to Taiwan, Rita Joyce Duke, gave the following testimony about her experiences in Sunbeam Band and in Girls' Auxiliary:

As soon as we children were old enough we joined the WMU and became active members of the Sunbeam Band. It was there that I began hearing about home and foreign missions, but this area seemed far removed from me.

As a Junior GA, I attended an associational GA meeting in my home church, where a missionary from Africa was the main speaker. I sat on the front row to observe this 'strange creature.' I listened attentively to everything she said and was thrilled beyond words. After the meeting I rushed home to tell the family that I was going to be a missionary to Africa. Their response was not discouraging; they didn't act at all surprised. It was sometime later that Mother revealed that she had wanted to go as a missionary but since it wasn't God's will she had prayed that one of her children would go.

Beyond assisting persons to hear God's call to vocational missionary service, Woman's Missionary Union makes a continuing contribution by helping every Christian to find and to express his basic missionary responsibility. Not every Christian can go to a missions field in another part of the

United States or the world, but every Christian can fulfil his missionary responsibility.

The three broad areas of action in the WMU task of leading persons to participate in missions are praying for missions, giving for the support of missions, and witnessing and ministering through mission action. In engaging persons in these actions, Woman's Missionary Union helps develop in them a growing response to their responsibility to proclaim the gospel and to minister to human need in Christ's name in all the world.

1. *Praying for Missions*

The missionary movement was born in prayer. The apostles depended upon the prayer life of the church for stimulus and power. The book of Acts reminds twentieth-century Christians of the place given to united prayer in the expansion of the kingdom. The early Christians knew how to pray. They were willing to wait with one accord in prayer for God to speak to them. And he spoke.

Through prayer the churches of Britain were prepared to accept William Carey's challenge and the resulting missionary enterprise. The prayer meeting under the haystack at Williams College started American churches on their adventure in world missions. And there are multitudes today who support the missionary work of a church through prayer. Except for prayer, missions would die.

Prayer is the means by which the power of God is brought to bear upon the missions task. Not all Christians can go to missions fields in other lands or in other parts of the United States, but all can be missionaries through prayer.

Through prayer, untrained hands can perform operations in hospitals all over the world.

Through prayer, tongues that speak only one language can tell the story of Jesus in many languages.

One missionary wrote home to say, "Today, you and I won a Chinese woman to Christ. And, you helped me teach little children to sing 'Jesus Loves Me.' You were standing right by my side with your prayers." Through prayer Christians can work side by side with missionaries around the world. Through prayer Christians are empowered to witness and to minister every day.

After Frank Laubach had spoken to a large audience on the subject "Prayer, the Mightiest Force in the World," a woman came from the audience and asked Dr. Laubach this question: "If prayer is the mightiest force in the world, why haven't the prayers of Christians done more to change the world?" Dr. Laubach replied, "Because their prayers have been a trickle when they should have been a river."

What a responsibility every church has to make its members aware of the potential of prayer! Church members need to break out of the narrow circle of interest which engulfs them and open their hearts to the cries of a world. Woman's Missionary Union helps enlarge the sphere of this concern in a church and guides in intercessory prayer for all people who are oppressed, hungry, fearful, and lost.

Effective prayer is rooted in an understanding of the biblical teachings about prayer. An understanding of the biblical teachings about prayer includes its authority in the Scriptures, its scope, its purpose, its results, its possibilities. From learning about prayer, the Christian moves to the experience of prayer. In moments of private and public intercession, God's power is released. Those who pray and those who are prayed for are blessed. Missions demands more than the often heard prayer, "Bless all the missionaries on the foreign fields."

Many persons are living at so fast a pace they are too busy to pray. Christ gave all Christians an example of a dynamic prayer life. He withdrew to quiet places for meditation and prayer. If he needed such hours, how much more do Christians of the twentieth century need them!

The followers of Jesus learned well the lesson of prayer. Pentecost came after ten days of waiting and prayer, and the Holy Spirit came to abide in his church as he had come to abide with Christians. After Pentecost, the Scriptures record that the rapidly growing church "continued steadfastly in . . . prayer." When persecution came, the church prayed.

The life of the apostle Paul illustrates the power of prayer in his ministry. He and his converts engaged in mutual prayer support. He was always praying for them. "Now I pray to God that ye do no evil" (2 Cor. 13:7). "We pray always for you, that our God would count you worthy of this calling" (2 Thess. 1:11). And Paul always pleaded for the prayers of others in his behalf: "Continue steadfastly in prayer, . . . and pray for us also, that God may open to us a door for the word" (Col. 4:2, RSV). "Pray for us, that the word of the Lord may run and be glorified" (2 Thess. 3:1, ASV). All that Paul did was planned and permeated by prayer, and his missionary endeavors were projected upon the power of it. He affirmed what present-day Christians sometimes forget—that prayer is the first and greatest secret of success in kingdom work.

The call to prayer is relevant in every age. Baker James Cauthen, executive secretary of the Foreign Mission Board, speaking of the challenge in missions, bared his heart to the burden of advance and the corresponding power necessary to effect it:

> Advance [in missions] will call for growth on all fronts. It cannot be done unilaterally. A new horizon in foreign missions can never be attained apart from growth at the home base in evangelism, church extension, Christian education, theological training, and every aspect of church development. A new tide of spiritual growth must come in and lift us up into new dimensions. The expression of this growth will be a new forward

thrust in missions—into the many lands where we now serve and into others that ought to be entered.

The chief requisite for this new thrust is a new experience of spiritual power. We must move in the direction of a depth approach in world missions. It calls for deep repentance, soul searching, revitalization of prayer, and seeking the power of the Holy Spirit. We must keep in mind that the Lord of the harvest, himself, must thrust out the laborers into the harvest. We must pray that we shall be filled with the Holy Spirit so that our labor may have his divine, sharp-cutting edge.

We must regard ourselves as laborers together with God—not laboring in our own strength, but God at work in us. If we yield ourselves to his leadership, sovereignty, and divine power, we may discover that in the closing decades of the twentieth century will be written a story of Christian witness in spiritual victory to the glory of Jesus Christ.

A vital dimension, then, to the work of Woman's Missionary Union is the leading of persons to participate in missions through a vital intercessory prayer experience on behalf of missions. In this way Woman's Missionary Union makes another essential contribution to the life and work of a church.

2. *Giving for the Support of Missions*

Someone asked the great preacher Phillips Brooks what he would first do if he were called to be pastor of a broken-down church—a church that had lost its building, was not able to support a pastor, and was torn by internal dissension. He hesitated for a moment and then replied: "I should get all the people together, preach the greatest sermon I could on worldwide missions, and take the best offering I could get for the work in heathen lands." A person commenting on Mr. Brooks's statement said, "The church needs the world to redeem it from selfishness."

The kingdom of God can never be built by money alone, but financial support is essential. Every church is under solemn obligation to instruct its members faithfully in the worldwide meaning of their faith and in the high privilege and duty of using material resources for the widest expansion of the gospel to the whole world.

Christians must match the hour in which they live, or they will fail God and humanity. The rapid growth of the population of the world has led statisticians to make the prediction that at the present rate of giving money and personnel only about 20 percent of the world's population will profess to be Christian by the year 2000. The need for churches, hospitals, and schools is urgent. World missions cannot wait. The world will remain lost to the forces of evil unless Christians come to accept and to practice Christian stewardship with all its implications.

The stewardship of material possessions is one of the central teachings of the New Testament. Nothing a Christian possesses is his very own personal property (Acts 4:32). All things belong to God and redeemed men are his stewards to use these resources for his purposes.

Each Christian must measure his giving in terms of his capacity to aid his fellowmen in Jesus' name. Above all, there must be the conviction developed by prayer and Bible study as to what the Lord would have him do. There are many biblical teachings which undergird stewardship of possessions. Some of these are:

All I have belongs to God; my life and all my income are a trust from God to be used as he directs (James 1:17).

I must give an account to God for my use of everything I possess (Rom. 14:12).

I am to give through my church regularly, liberally, cheerfully, sacrificially (Mal. 3:10).

I am to conquer covetousness and to lay up eternal treasures (Matt. 6:19–21).

I am to be motivated by love in all my giving (1 John 5:2).

The sacrifice of some who give themselves in mission service should be matched by the sacrificial giving of those who serve at home. A time of renewed missionary concern will be reflected by liberal gifts to missions causes.

When Jesus met Peter by the seashore in the early morning hours after the resurrection, he asked Peter: "Lovest thou me?" Peter replied: "Yea, Lord, thou knowest that I love Thee." Three times Jesus asked the question, and three times Peter gave the answer, but each time upon Peter's protest of love Jesus laid the stewardship obligation of life: "Feed my lambs." "Feed my sheep." "Feed my sheep."

God teaches in his Word that those who have received his material blessings are to share those blessings with others. This sharing should not issue from a stern sense of duty but rather from motivation impelled by the power of love. Until giving is spontaneous and joyful, church members will be tempted to reduce the amount of their giving as much as they can without entirely refusing to give.

Woman's Missionary Union gives attention to the tithe as a basic requirement for giving and emphasizes giving beyond the tithe in the form of missions offerings. The church is recognized as the storehouse, and attention is given in Woman's Missionary Union to helping church members evaluate ways their church spends its money, particularly in relationship to world missions. Local needs and local budgets ought never to be given primacy over the great cause of the evangelization of the world. Neglecting the Great Commission under the pretext of local obligation is missing the very genius of Christianity.

WMU also interprets the Cooperative Program as the channel of giving for Southern Baptists. The Cooperative Program has often been called the lifeline of missions. Without this efficient denominational plan of financial support of missions work at home and abroad, the world missions program of Southern Baptists would suffer immeasurably. The Cooperative Program enables every member of a church to have a part in all that his state convention and the Southern Baptist Convention are doing. This plan makes participation by members and by churches worldwide in scope.

One pastor describes the missionary dollar given through the Cooperative Program in this way:

A missionary dollar is concentrated compassion.

A missionary dollar is the word on the wing to jungle bypaths, and villages presided over by Fuji, and traffic-jammed cities noisy with perishing people.

The missionary dollar is a sword stroke against the evil powers that do battle against God and the godly.

The missionary dollar is the essence of "me," going with the gospel where the bodily "me" cannot go.

My missionary dollar is tongues telling, hands healing, lives living for Jesus wherever the missionaries serve.

The Cooperative Program enables us to reach around the world with our missionary dollars.[3]

Woman's Missionary Union encourages church members to use their influence to help their churches see missions needs beyond themselves and to have a part in the world missions program by proper sharing of the money received.

Each individual should know not only how the Cooperative Program works but also how much his church is contributing to missions through this channel. Alma Hunt, in the book *Woman's Missionary Union,* points out that the ultimate answer as to how much an individual gives through the Cooperative Program depends upon three decisions arrived at by the Baptist democratic process of action: (1) The vote of the church as to the percentage to be given through the Cooperative Program; (2) the vote of the state convention as to the percentage received from the churches to be used in the state and the percentage to be forwarded for Southern Baptist Convention causes, also the vote of the state convention as to the distribution of its state funds; and (3) the vote of the Southern Baptist Convention as to the distribution of its funds.

A prerequisite to generous giving is an acceptance of the tithe as the basic plan of giving, the church budget as the management of the church members' gifts, and the Cooperative Program as a channel of giving to all Southern Baptist Convention causes. Beyond this, churches must provide opportunities for members to make offerings over and above the tithe for the support of a cause which is large enough to demand the very best from every Christian.

3. *Witnessing and Ministering Through Mission Action*

Mission action is the organized effort of a church to extend its ministry and witness to persons of special need or circumstance not presently enrolled or immediate prospects for membership in the church or its organizations.

No Christian has the right to expect to be able to live effectively in a worldwide context unless he has begun to live effectively in the smaller world of his community and home. No program of missionary education has the right to expect to be fruitful in its worldwide implications unless it first proves itself so in its local setting. Nothing is so likely to inject life into the total program of a church as an honest facing of local conditions and an earnest attempt to meet them in the spirit of Christ. Growth in the concept of missions as being worldwide in scope begins with an understanding of missions needs in one's community.

As important as praying and giving are, a severe test of missionary concern comes at the point of service where one is. In WMU this area of responsibility has been called personal service, community missions, or Christian witnessing. More recently the term "mission action" has been used. This work reminds members of a church that the fulfilling of the Great Commission begins in the community where the church is located. Most church members will not go to Japan or Indonesia or Europe to proclaim the gospel and to minister to human need, but they do have the privilege of proclaiming and ministering next door. How a church member measures up to this responsibility tests the genuineness of his missions concern.

Christ was concerned first with motivation, then with method. He implored his disciples: "Look! I tell you, lift up your eyes and scan the fields, for they are already white for harvesting" (John 4:35, Williams). Genuine zeal for witnessing needs to be cultivated. Then it must be reinforced by action.

The commission which prompted Lottie Moon to go to China, which prompts missionaries to go to Africa, and which sends missionaries to an Indian reservation in Arizona is the same commission that sends church members down the street or across town to witness and to minister to a neighbor. Christ says to all Christians "Go": go to the next house, to the next street, to the next town, to the next city, to the islands of the sea. Each church member cannot go to all these places, but he can send missionaries and support them with his prayers and gifts. But in the place where he can go, he can witness and minister.

One of the most thrilling features of the missionary enterprise is the absolute immediacy of the task. Every church has a missions field within its reach. This is why Woman's Missionary Union, in leading persons to participate in missions, feels a keen sense of responsibility for leading church members to witness and to minister through missionary activities.

Hugo Culpepper, director of the Missions Division of

the Home Mission Board, has made the following observation concerning the need for mission action in the community: "As never before, the effectiveness of our world outreach is dependent on what we are becoming and doing here at home! Southern Baptists themselves are being weighed in the balances today. Unless we permit the grace of God to redeem us, we have no message for the world as to the power of the gospel. It is not enough to verbalize the gospel, especially if one knows little about it in terms of redemptive experience. Our message must be authentic as an expression of God's grace working through us on its way to others; it must also be *relevant* to needs of people in their total personality and in their life situation. It must be both personal and social in its application and effect. From this perspective, community missions and home missions constitute one of the most challenging frontiers for Southern Baptists in our time."[4]

Woman's Missionary Union and Brotherhood serve Christ and assist his church by leading in a program of mission action in the community. The following are examples of individuals and groups whose needs can be met through mission action:

Language and cultural minorities (Indians, Latin-Americans, Orientals, Europeans, Jewish, international students)

Physically handicapped (blind, deaf, retarded)

Socially handicapped (underprivileged, migrants, transients, illiterates, juvenile delinquents, imprisoned, parolees, ex-prisoners, alcoholics, unwed mothers)

Persons in institutions (rest homes, hospitals)

Persons in military service

Persons in areas where the organization of a church is impossible.

Meeting the needs of these people will require a variety of activities.

Some of these activities may include:

Conducting mission Sunday Schools, mission Bible classes, and mission Vacation Bible Schools

Engaging in personal ministries based on individual needs

Establishing or assisting with mission-center type work (club work, recreational activities, child care, medical clinics, occupational and vocational assistance)

Distributing Bibles and Christian literature

Conducting projects to combat moral problems in the community.

Persons of special need or circumstance will not be reached for a church unless they are given special attention. The activities of a church in reaching prospects often miss these groups of people who require not only a witness but also a ministry in the name of Jesus Christ. Mission action combines the elements of witness and ministry into a missionary approach for reaching these people.

Approaches being made to mission action in the community are the same ones being made in missions work in other parts of the world, as borders and barriers are crossed in fulfilling the missions task.

How did Southern Baptist missionaries enter Indonesia? They built a hospital in Kediri to meet the physical needs of people and through this means established and extended a Christian witness. One of the reasons missions work is strong in Africa today is that missionaries established schools to meet a need for education, and they combined with this ministry an effective witness. Combinations of ministry and witness are needed in every community. This combination is at the very heart of the idea of mission action.

Christ's followers today need the same power that the apostles had after the day of Pentecost. Christians today have the same gospel to preach that the apostles preached.

They have an unbelieving world as their missions field, just as the apostles had. There are the same basic sins to meet that the early Christians met. The same basic human nature exists. There have been no fundamental changes in any of these things from the time of Christ until now. Without the Spirit's presence and power the most heroic efforts will fail; with his Spirit and his power, the most humble endeavors will succeed.

In 1 John 3, the burden of the world's need is laid upon Christians. John intimates that it is impossible for God's love to dwell in a heart that possesses material wealth but is closed to those in need. In chapter 4 follows love's final appeal, based on the love of God, who sent his Son into the world that man might live through him. Because of his love, men ought to love one another. Therefore, the question that every Christian must face squarely is this: Do I love Christ enough to share that which I possess—with the hungry, that they may be fed; with the naked, that they may be clothed; with the sick, that they may be healed; with the imprisoned, that they may know his blessed ministry; and with the lost, that they may be saved?

Through mission action, Woman's Missionary Union helps lead a church out into the world where its ministry is to be received by masses of people.

IV. RELATIONSHIPS IN PARTICIPATION IN MISSIONS

Just as there are important relationships among church program organizations in the teaching tasks of a church, there are also important relationships among these organizations in performance tasks or doing the work of a church.

1. Woman's Missionary Union and Brotherhood

The missions organizations for men and women in a church share a parallel role in leading the church to participate in missions. Certain responsibilities are held in common by both organizations: praying for missions, giving for the support of missions, and mission action. By working together these two organizations can reach the entire church membership and engage church members in activities in behalf of missions. Although each organization is responsible for its own program, there are many opportunities for the two organizations to work together.

2. Woman's Missionary Union and Sunday School

The Sunday School has the task of leading all church members to worship daily. As the Sunday School leads members to experience worship daily, Woman's Missionary Union adds another dimension by encouraging intercessory prayer for missions as a part of this daily worship experience. WMU provides guides for individual, family, and corporate prayer for missions.

Both Woman's Missionary Union and Sunday School have tasks relating to ministry and witness. Woman's Missionary Union is responsible for witnessing and ministering in its task: Lead persons to participate in missions. The Sunday School has responsibilities spelled out in its task: Lead all church members to worship, witness, learn, and minister daily. There is a distinctive contribution, however, which each organization makes in these areas of work.

WMU plays a supporting role to the efforts of Sunday School in leading all persons to witness daily. WMU cooperates in the witnessing program planned by the Sunday School and offers an action-inducing curriculum which guides members to take advantage of witnessing opportunities growing out of daily contacts in the home and community.

Sunday School also has the task: Lead all persons to minister daily. Ministry actions can be spontaneous or planned;

they may be extended to church members or nonchurch members. The Sunday School ministers primarily to the church constituency. Because of the weekly meetings of Sunday School and the closely graded groups, the units of a Sunday School can rally quickly to meet the needs of persons with whom members have contact. WMU ministers primarily to persons of special need or circumstance through mission action. Discovering needs, planning, conducting, and evaluating this mission action ministry is the work of Woman's Missionary Union. The ministry program of WMU includes types of work being promoted by the Home Mission Board, as well as other church-related work.

While the Sunday School is leading persons to witness and minister, Woman's Missionary Union will be planning mission action efforts in the community which unite witness and ministry into a single missions thrust. This adds another dimension to the work being done by Sunday School.

Sunday School and Woman's Missionary Union also relate in the work of outreach. The Sunday School has the task: Lead in reaching all prospects for the church. In leading a church to reach prospects, the Sunday School spends its major time on a more or less direct approach to outreach. This approach involves discovering prospects, visiting them, bringing them to the church, witnessing to them, and reaching them for church membership. But in this direct approach to reaching people, many groups of people with special need or living in special circumstances are often overlooked. It is primarily these persons whom Woman's Missionary Union attempts to reach for Christ and for his church through its program of mission action.

3. *Woman's Missionary Union and Training Union*

Training Union has the task: Train church members to perform the functions of their church (worship, minister, proclaim, educate). This places upon Training Union the responsibility for equipping church members with the skills necessary to carry on the work of the church. Woman's Missionary Union leads church members to engage in certain types of work in behalf of the church: prayer, giving, and mission action. These kinds of work require skills for performance. A person needs to learn such skills as how to witness, how to worship through giving, how to visit in an institution. The WMU works alongside Training Union in making Training Union aware of the skills needed to perform certain types of work. The Training Union gives training to church members so they are equipped to carry on the work they are being led to do by the Woman's Missionary Union.

4. Woman's Missionary Union and Missions Committee

A church can call upon its missions committee to assume certain responsibilities relating to missions work. This committee assists the church in discovering possibilities for local missions projects and in sharing findings with church program organizations through the church council. In missions work requiring heavy administrative responsibilities relating to facilities, finances, and/or employed personnel, the missions committee should give leadership to the work and appropriately involve WMU and Brotherhood. This work is also coordinated in the church council.

Relationships can be summarized as follows: The major resources of other church program organizations are spent helping a church realize its mission in its immediate area—reaching all prospects for a church, leading church members to perform the functions of the church, and training them in this performance. Woman's Missionary Union and Brotherhood assist a church by leading it to an awareness and a response to the mission of the church beyond its immediate witness, to the end of the world. But, in order to keep the "far-off" view of missions in perspective, Woman's Missionary Union engages persons in witness and ministry activities locally to keep missions concern intensely practical in terms of personal involvement and to help a church be missionary where it is located.

CHAPTER 4

I. Conducting Special Projects
   1. Characteristics of Special Projects
      (1) Short-term
      (2) Relate to Ongoing Program
      (3) Support Ongoing Program
   2. Special Projects Conducted by WMU
      (1) Missions Offering Projects
      (2) Prayer Projects
      (3) Other Projects
   3. Relationships in Conducting Special Projects

II. Channeling Information
   1. Need for an Informed Church
   2. WMU—A Channel of Communication
      (1) Interpreting the Work of the Church
      (2) Interpreting the Work of the Denomination

4

Serving the Church and the Denomination

WHILE each church program organization has distinctive tasks to perform, there are two tasks which all organizations share. These tasks are: (1) provide organization and leadership for special projects of the church, and (2) provide and interpret information regarding the work of the church and denomination.

These two tasks are sometimes referred to in an abbreviated form as a special projects task and a channeling task. These tasks represent two special areas of work in which organizations can engage for a church and the denomination. These tasks signify the availability of church organizations to perform special services a church needs.

I. CONDUCTING SPECIAL PROJECTS

Some activities in the life of the church may be referred to as basic and ongoing. These activities take place week in and week out, month in and month out, year in and year out. They are basic because they are essential if the church accomplishes its objectives. They are ongoing because of their essential nature. The first two tasks of Woman's Missionary Union represent basic, ongoing activities. "Teach missions" and "lead persons to participate in missions" are basic activities which must go on all the time if a church is to fulfil its world missions task.

These basic and continuing activities must not only take

place but also involve all church members. As long as the missionary activity of a church is the concern of only a few of the members, a church cannot hope to measure up to its responsibility. All the members of a church should seek to understand their church's missionary responsibility, to purify their church's motives concerning missions, and to equip their church for its missions task.

A church should attempt to reach all members in its program of missionary education. Special missions projects intensify the participation and contribution of all church members in the missions task. Church missions projects may also help involve more of the church members in missions. Some church members who might never be reached otherwise are reached through projects.

1. *Characteristics of Special Projects*

There are three major characteristics which identify special projects.

(1) SHORT-TERM

Special projects come at a point in time in a church's program. Projects have a distinguishable beginning time and ending time; they are short in duration. They issue from a decision on the part of a church to focus attention for a period of time on a significant area of its work.

(2) RELATE TO ONGOING PROGRAM

As a church decides on the basic work it is to do, designates this work as tasks to be performed, and assigns tasks to church program organizations for performance, a church sets into motion its basic, ongoing program of work. The performance of these tasks constitutes the fundamental work of all organizations. "Teach missions," for example, is a basic church task performed by WMU.

While performance of tasks goes on all the time, it is desirable to lift out segments of the ongoing work and focus special attention on them. When a segment of work is singled out for special emphasis, the emphasis is called a project. An example of a project is the Lottie Moon Christmas Offering for Foreign Missions. Woman's Missionary Union emphasizes praying for missions and giving for the support of missions on a continuing basis as it seeks to lead persons to participate in missions. But each December WMU leads in planning for this special project which accents giving to missions. The Lottie Moon Christmas Offering comes at a point in time, focuses attention on giving, and adds emphasis to this part of a church's work. The project relates to the ongoing program of missionary education and action, but it is a special project because of its focus and duration. All the projects conducted by a church will grow out of and relate to the church's basic, continuing work.

(3) SUPPORT ONGOING PROGRAM

A special project gives new impetus or new thrust to the ongoing program of work in a church. An excellent example of this can be found in the area of evangelism. The Sunday School is constantly leading a church in the area of evangelism through outreach and witness. At a point in time, however, a church may decide to have a revival. A revival is a special project. The revival has a distinguishable beginning time and ending time; it grows out of the sustained program of evangelism; and it supports or gives new impetus to that program.

By assuming responsibility for the special projects task, Woman's Missionary Union says to a church: This organization is at your disposal; leaders and members stand ready to do the important jobs the church wants done. Woman's Missionary Union and Brotherhood have supporting roles in all projects, but they take the lead in conducting missions projects since these organizations have continuing responsibilities relating to missions.

2. *Special Projects Conducted by WMU*

There are several missions projects for which Woman's Missionary Union can provide organization and leadership. These missions projects relate to studying missions, giving for the support of missions, praying for missions, and witnessing and ministering through mission action in the community. These aspects of the basic program of Woman's Missionary Union furnish the substance out of which missions projects may be formed.

Some of the well-known missions projects conducted by Woman's Missionary Union are discussed below. A church may initiate other projects as they are needed and through the church council assign them to Woman's Missionary Union.

(1) MISSIONS OFFERING PROJECTS

Missions offerings in behalf of home and foreign missions are well-known projects for which Woman's Missionary Union provides organization and leadership. These special offerings came into being in response to the needs of a lost world, and God has given Baptist missions work remarkable stimulation through them. Throughout its history Woman's Missionary Union has prayed and worked for increased missions giving. The growth of the missions offerings from a very small beginning to the greater place they now hold in meeting world need is evidence of answered prayer beyond what any person might have dared to hope.

These missions offerings are the Lottie Moon Christmas Offering for Foreign Missions and the Annie Armstrong Offering for Home Missions. The foreign missions offering is taken in December each year, and the home missions offering is taken in March. The objective of these offerings is not to call attention to the organization that nurtures them but to provide financial resources so that the gospel may be shared with the whole world.

These offerings make possible participation in missions by a greater number of Southern Baptists. In thousands of churches throughout the Southern Baptist fellowship the entire church family has discovered the blessing and joy of giving to these missions offerings. The offerings have grown year by year with an increasing involvement on the part of the total church membership.

The missions offerings are results of prayer. The offerings could not be understood completely apart from the weeks of prayer. The offerings grow out of prayer in behalf of missions. The weeks of prayer are spiritual forces in Baptist life. The prayers of Southern Baptists added to the gifts bring blessings which money alone could never provide.

The offerings are tied securely not only to prayer but also to study. In study the needs of the world are called to the attention of church members as information is shared about the efforts being made to meet these needs in Christ's name. The hearts of church members are touched, and they respond when they know human need and recognize what Christ expects of each Christian. In their preaching, many pastors set forth the biblical basis of missions and the duties of a church and every Christian in missions.

Missions offerings meet critical needs around the world. Requests for funds are drawn up in prayer and careful study by missionaries in the United States and abroad and are approved by the Home Mission Board and the Foreign Mission Board. The needs always exceed the resources of the mission boards. Many urgent needs such as church buildings, schools, and hospitals are forced to wait because funds are not adequate. Through the years the Lottie Moon Christmas Offering and the Annie Armstrong Offering have made available additional funds. In fact, these gifts of Southern Baptists provide almost one half of the support of the foreign and home missions programs of Southern Baptists.

Missions offerings reinforce the Cooperative Program. The Cooperative Program, the denominational channel of support for missions, has been called the lifeline of the world missions program of Southern Baptists. It must always be a basic means of support for missions work. Missions offerings reinforce and undergird this basic means of support. Baker James Cauthen said:

> Through the Lottie Moon offering are opened fountains of missionary compassion which continue to flow freely throughout the year. Missionary conviction is a continuing matter. When the Spirit of God leads a person to see his missionary responsibilities, he cannot stop with a gift to an offering. He must become a steward of his possessions throughout the year. . . . The Cooperative Program must continually widen and deepen as a channel through which missionary compassion can flow to a lost world. The vast missionary conviction which comes through the Lottie Moon offering is of highest significance in helping churches catch a vision of sharing an ever increasing percentage of the money laid upon the altar that the rest of the world may know Christ.[1]

One of the greatest benefits of missions offerings is their challenge to life dedication. As young people study, pray, and give, they are brought face to face with the question of giving their own lives in behalf of missions. Pastors and other church leaders often find Christ directing them to missions fields while praying for and encouraging giving to these offerings.

(2) PRAYER PROJECTS

Growing out of its ongoing emphasis on intercessory prayer in behalf of missions, Woman's Missionary Union provides organization and leadership for significant prayer projects in the life of the church. Three illustrations of the types of activity in this area are weeks of prayer, prayer retreats, and special prayer meetings.

The practice of intercessory prayer gives Christians the assurance that they enter into God's plan for world evangelism as "laborers together with God." Woman's Missionary Union has recognized that prayer must have first place in the missionary enterprise if the commission of Christ is to be realized. This emphasis on prayer grows even stronger as a church is confronted by the urgency of world needs. A Southern Baptist missionary pleaded: "Please back every dollar you have given with earnest prayer that Christ may be known throughout the whole world."

The privilege and the responsibility of prayer calls church members aside for special prayer in behalf of missions. The best known church prayer projects in behalf of missions are the Week of Prayer for Home Missions in March and the Week of Prayer for Foreign Missions in December. During the Home Mission Week of Prayer and the Foreign Mission Week of Prayer, members of the church put aside other consuming interests and give attention to the work God is guiding Southern Baptists to do in missions. Members gain information which forms an adequate basis for concern. They pray with renewed devotion for missions work around the world. These elements of study and prayer combine to motivate generous giving to the missions offerings in behalf of home and foreign missions. No one activity for which Woman's Missionary Union can provide organization and leadership is more important in the life of the church than the weeks of prayer. Through these intensive prayer experiences, the power of God can be released, and a church's influence can be extended around the world.

Another special prayer project is a prayer retreat. The prayer retreat provides time and opportunity to withdraw from daily distractions and seek the will of God through a study of the Scriptures and prayer. A prayer retreat may lead to self-examination, repentance, and a deepening of faith. In a world of confusion and stress, Christians need to find time to gather in Christ's name and to seek his leadership in the solution of their problems. Communing with God for the purpose of knowing him better and loving him more should be the aim of all prayer retreats.

Today, as in the days when Jesus was on earth and spoke to a small group of disciples, he gives us this assurance: "Where two or three are gathered together in my name, there am I in the midst of them" (Matt. 18:20).

A retreat, held in a quiet place as free as possible from interruptions, creates an atmosphere conducive to worship. The important element in planning a retreat is not the length of time, but the manner in which the time is spent. The entire time should be given to prayer and communion with God. Elements of worship may be more meaningful in the retreat atmosphere: Scripture reading, hymns, Bible study, discussions, individual meditation, sharing of Christian experiences, seasons of prayer and intercession, reading, group meditation. Missions needs around the world are always a major concern in one of these experiences.

WMU also can conduct special prayer meetings for a church. These may be prerevival prayer services or prayer services in the interest of other special emphases in the church.

(3) OTHER PROJECTS

Based on the definition that projects grow out of the basic and ongoing work of an organization, there are two other types of projects for which Woman's Missionary Union can provide organization and leadership. These are projects in the areas of mission study and mission action.

While the study of missions is going on weekly or monthly in Woman's Missionary Union organizations, it would be appropriate for a church to decide to have a special project in mission study. Woman's Missionary Union could provide the organization and leadership for such a study. Interesting possibilities for study projects exist. Each year a graded series of books on foreign missions and a graded series on home missions is produced for study in churches. It is possible for a church to allow this study to become a church-wide project in mission study.

Other special projects relating to mission action can be conducted. Woman's Missionary Union attempts to aid the church by carrying on an ongoing program of mission action; to undergird this there are also opportunities for special community missions projects. Sponsoring or conducting a mission Vacation Bible School in a city or rural area is one example.

Other possibilities exist for carrying out service projects in behalf of missions work—local, state, United States, or world. In a service project, material assistance is provided to meet specific needs. This might include the collection of clothing to meet the needs of refugees in any part of the world. Service projects include such things as furnishing food and bedding for a rescue mission in the community or association; helping to meet an emergency when a disaster strikes; making layettes for new babies in the charity ward of a hospital; collecting medical supplies for a hospital overseas. These are project-type activities which are not carried on all the time, but ones which can release tremendous assistance to missions efforts locally and around the world.

Woman's Missionary Union is equipped to handle these projects and others which the church may feel are its opportunities. Woman's Missionary Union includes four age-level units: Woman's Missionary Society, Young Woman's Auxiliary, Girls' Auxiliary, and Sunbeam Band. Members of these organizations can be quickly mobilized to get important jobs done for the church. Woman's Missionary Union also has leaders trained in the skills of doing the basic missions work of a church. The energies and abilities of these leaders can be directed toward fulfilling specific things a church wants to accomplish. Woman's Missionary Union has the resource of the time of its meetings, which can be given to assist the church. And, above all, Woman's Missionary Union has a sense of mission about its place of responsibility in a church and, because of this, is eager and ready to do in behalf of a church what needs to be done.

3. Relationships in Conducting Special Projects

Every church program organization is available to help the church with special projects. On many projects, all organizations will work together. Leadership for projects should be assigned to the organization or organizations whose primary purpose relates to the project. For example, the Training Union can assume the leadership for a training project. Woman's Missionary Union and Brotherhood can assume responsibility for missions projects. Other church program organizations play a supporting role. These relationships are worked out in the church council, where leaders of the church program organizations work together in planning a coordinated church program.

In a missions offering project, for example, Woman's Missionary Union and Brotherhood take the lead in providing organization and leadership. As Woman's Missionary Union and Brotherhood give leadership to the project, other organizations play supporting roles. The Sunday School serves as a channel of communication, using department assemblies to interpret the need for the missions offering. Sunday School may provide one channel for collecting the offering. The Training Union reinforces the effort by communicating information regarding the project. Another dimension to be added by Training Union might also be the training of a group of workers to interpret in meetings of the church the need for the offering. The Music Ministry lends its support by providing music appropriate to the emphasis.

Another illustration of relationship can be seen in mission action projects. Woman's Missionary Union and Brotherhood provide the leadership for such projects. Sunday School, through teaching the biblical revelation, helps provide motivation for participation in the projects and provides specific information to interpret these projects to members of the church enrolled in Sunday School. The Training Union provides training in developing the skills that people need to engage effectively in the projects.

A tremendous force is at the disposal of every church as it relates its organizations together to get significant jobs done. Through proper relationships the organizations work as a team: the efforts of one complementing the efforts of another, the strengths of one supplementing the strengths of another, the spirit of one permeating the spirit of another, until the full resources and energies of a church are directed toward common goals and purposes. When church program organizations work as a team, each contributes a distinctive share to the total task. There seems to be no limit to what a church can accomplish through its organizations as they work together under the leadership of the Holy Spirit.

II. CHANNELING INFORMATION

Another task shared by the church program organizations is to provide and interpret information regarding the work of the church and the denomination. This is a communications task. Through this task each church program organization commits itself to serve as a channel of communication for the church and the denomination.

1. *Need for an Informed Church*

Communication is essential in a church. An informed church is well on its way to being prepared to fulfil its mission in the world. Informed church members are more likely to be involved in the life and work of a church. Informed church organizations are more likely to support the major work a church wants to accomplish.

Communication is persons expressing themselves, talking with one another, exchanging ideas, and sharing feelings. Communication is the process whereby ideas and beliefs are shared with others. Communication is two-way; it involves not only speaking but also listening.

Communication begins with the acknowledgment of another person or another group. In the physical sense, this means seeing, noticing, welcoming, and making room for the person or group. In a deeper sense it means hearing, paying attention to, being receptive to and appreciative of the responses of the person or group. It means speaking the language of the other person or group. Communication suggests mutual support, respect, and understanding.

Nothing is more tragic than a breakdown in communication. A family situation becomes miserable when members of a family cease to talk and to listen to one another. When a husband goes his way, a wife goes her way, and the children go their way without free and open sharing, family life breaks down. The same thing can happen in a church family. When church members do not share common goals, when organizations do not exist to serve common purposes, and when there is very little communication among church members and among church organizations, there can be a breakdown in relationships within the church. Frustrations occur, conflicts occur, losses of energy occur. The church is no longer united in its endeavors. It lacks the united thrust and positive influence it should be having in the world.

Information flows among persons and groups in a church through formal as well as informal means. Informally, members of the church and organizations of the church communicate with one another. To supplement this type, the church must also have formal means of communication to insure that information is transmitted to persons and groups who need it. In this sense, communication must be planned for.

Planning for communication is the design of the task: Provide and interpret information regarding the work of the church and the denomination. This task to be performed by each church program organization represents a deliberate attempt on the part of the church to communicate effectively its plans and work.

A church communicates in many ways. The pastor communicates through his sermon and announcements. There is communication through bulletins, newspapers, letters, and promotional media. A major means of communication open to the church is its organizations. Organizations serve as effective means of communication when the leaders of these organizations carry information about the work of the church and the denomination to the members of the organizations.

In a sense, church organizations may be thought of as channels. A channel is that through which something passes, a conduit through which something flows. Church program organizations should serve the church by being channels through which information flows.

2. WMU—A Channel of Communication

A large segment of a church's membership is enlisted in WMU age-level organizations. Leaders of Woman's Missionary Union can communicate to these members information regarding the work of the church and denomination.

(1) INTERPRETING THE WORK OF THE CHURCH

Woman's Missionary Union channels information concerning the work of a church in several ways. One way is through study materials. Through studies in Woman's Missionary Society, Young Woman's Auxiliary, Girls' Auxiliary, and

Sunbeam Band, Woman's Missionary Union channels information about missions. The information which comes through study in organizational meetings, mission study books, magazine articles and features, and other ways is information the church needs to get to its members. Task I, Teach missions, expresses the basic channeling of missionary information by Woman's Missionary Union.

As members of Woman's Missionary Union receive information about missions and learn of their responsibility in missions, they are in a position to follow through and put into practice what they have learned. This is a part of the two-way communication process. A church has information to communicate, and a church needs participation in its work on the part of individual members. Therefore, the church communicates missions information through Woman's Missionary Union and, in turn, members of Woman's Missionary Union participate in the work of the church in missions. So, through study and other actions Woman's Missionary Union imparts missions information and gains the participation of church members in missions.

Another very valuable medium of communication is announcements and promotional features. The WMU president is a key to effective use of these two channels in behalf of the church. As the WMU president serves on the church council with other church leaders, she hears discussed the total plans of the church. She is present when the plans of the church program organizations are coordinated into a master plan for the church. She hears the concerns of the pastor expressed. She shares in the development of church objectives and goals. When she leaves the church council meeting, she is responsible for sharing this information with the members of Woman's Missionary Union. As she works with the leaders of Woman's Missionary Union—WMS presidents, YWA director, GA director, and Sunbeam Band director—she can communicate to these leaders the information regarding the plans of the church for the month or months ahead. They communicate this information to members of the organizations they lead.

The WMU president has the responsibility not only for communicating the work of Woman's Missionary Union but also the work of the total church as Woman's Missionary Union relates to it. When she views her responsibility as one part of a total church responsibility, she is in a position to grasp the importance of her relationship and to fulfil her role as a leader in the life of the church.

The WMU president shares information about the total church program with the members of Woman's Missionary Union, and she shares information about the plans and needs of Woman's Missionary Union with the congregation. She does this through church council meetings, in which she represents Woman's Missionary Union. She does this in congregational meetings of the church when she reports on the work of Woman's Missionary Union.

(2) INTERPRETING THE WORK OF THE DENOMINATION

Woman's Missionary Union also plays a significant role in interpreting the work of the denomination.

The denomination is represented by three major groups: the association, the state convention, and the Southern Baptist Convention. These exist for the purpose of assisting churches. These denominational groupings assist churches in one of two ways. They assist a church by providing it with materials and suggestions which will help it carry on its work in its immediate location, or they assist by doing for the church what it cannot do alone.

In the Southern Baptist Convention there are seventeen agencies which exist to assist churches. Examples of these agencies are Brotherhood Commission, Sunday School Board, Christian Life Commission, Stewardship Commission, Foreign Mission Board, and Home Mission Board.

Each of the agencies needs to communicate with a church. The agency desires either to communicate the assistance it has to give to a church or to communicate concerning the work it is doing in behalf of a church. For example, the Stewardship Commission wants to communicate the assistance it has to give churches in the area of stewardship, while the Foreign Mission Board wants to tell churches what it is doing for them in foreign missions.

Woman's Missionary Union in a church can serve as a church channel for carrying information to church members regarding the work of the denominational programs.

The church program organizations are Sunday School, Training Union, Woman's Missionary Union, Brotherhood, and Music Ministry. Each of these organizations has a supporting organization in the association, state convention, and Southern Baptist Convention. In the case of WMU, there is a church WMU, an associational WMU, a state WMU, and Woman's Missionary Union, Auxiliary to the Southern Baptist Convention. These organizations are known as channels because of the direct communication which they make possible among the churches, associations, states, and Southern Baptist Convention agencies.

There are many programs in the Southern Baptist Convention and in state conventions, however, that do not have corresponding organizations in a church. Yet these programs need a means of communicating with the church. They must either establish their own contacts with churches or make these contacts through established channels. These programs get much of their message to the church through the channel organizations. WMU serves as a channel in interpreting the work of the denomination.

Woman's Missionary Union on the Convention level assists the church WMU to be a channel of communication for the denomination. WMU magazines and other materials are used to interpret the work of other Southern Baptist Convention programs, such as the Christian Life Commission, the Radio and Television Commission, and the Baptist Joint Committee on Public Affairs. Feature stories, reports, and general articles in *Royal Service, The Window, Tell,* and *Sunbeam Activities* give women, young women, and children of the church a better understanding of their denomination.

Woman's Missionary Union on the Convention level also relies heavily on the resources of other programs in the development of its study and action programs. The informational services of the Home and Foreign Mission Boards are used in developing studies of contemporary missions for monthly organizational meetings. In this way WMU channels and communicates the work of the mission boards. Information about these mission boards is also built into mission study books and into the observance of the weeks of prayer.

In a very special way WMU channels some of the performance aspects of home missions. The Home Mission Board is aware that if America is won for Christ, each church must assume its share of the home missions task. The Home Mission Board appoints missionaries to do some of the work, but most of it must be done by churches. The mission action (community missions) phase of the WMU program channels many of the concerns of the Home Mission Board. The Home Mission Board develops the techniques for working with such groups as illiterates, migrants, and language groups; then WMU channels these techniques through its mission action plans.

WMU also relates to the stewardship program of the Convention. The Stewardship Commission was established to coordinate and to promote activities related to church finance and the Cooperative Program. Although states have promotional secretaries for stewardship, these secretaries do not have a special associational or church organization through which to work. Woman's Missionary Union in the church can both interpret the work of the Stewardship Commission and provide an educational base for its promotional activities.

In these and many other ways WMU provides and interprets information about the work of the denomination.

CHAPTER 5

5

Laboring Together

"TOGETHER" is a familiar word in the vocabulary of Woman's Missionary Union. The term appears in 1 Corinthians 3:9: "For we are labourers together with God." This passage of Scripture as the watchword of Woman's Missionary Union has served as a guide through the years.

"Together" is an interesting word. It implies combined action, agreement, and harmony. First Corinthians 3:9 is translated in many ways: "We are God's fellow-workers" (New English Bible); "We work together in God's service" (Moffatt); "For we are fellow-laborers for God" (Goodspeed). The Amplified New Testament translates the verse, "For we are fellow workmen—joint promoters, laborers together—with and for God."

The concept of laboring together applies to all of church life. As a church organizes to do its work, the several units work together. All of these units work to accomplish God's purpose for a church, but they do this by working with one another. Working together means working in partnership. Through proper relationship the organizations of a church and the leaders of a church work as a team. Team effort means mutual planning as ideas are shared. Teamwork implies that each job being done, each organization doing the work, and each person participating in planning the work are valuable to the total effort. The results of teamwork bring satisfaction to a larger number of persons. A person or an organization working in isolation fails to experience the spirit of teamwork and the results of a team effort.

A wise person once said:

> Coming together is beginning;
> keeping together is progress;
> thinking together is unity;
> working together is success.

I. Together in a Total Church Program

Woman's Missionary Union is one part of the total church program. There are other organizations of a church. There are other leaders. There is other work going on. As these work together in harmony and unity, a church is able to move forward to become the church God wants it to become.

A church may be compared to the human body. A healthy human body is coordinated. Each action is a means whereby the body expresses itself efficiently and effectively. A body not coordinated presents a tragic picture of disunity. When organizations of a church work together, the church can express itself effectively and efficiently.

A church program needs unity. Organizations of a church find their highest usefulness as they properly relate themselves to one another to reach church goals set under the leadership of the Holy Spirit. Working under the Holy Spirit's leadership implies dedication to God's purposes in the world. Working together in accomplishing these purposes is correlation and coordination.

In using the words "correlation" and "coordination," Southern Baptists are expressing a basic concept of working together. These words indicate that all the organizations of a church are brought together in proper relationship and that they work together in harmonious actions to help a church fulfil its mission. These two words are best understood when they are looked at along with the word "relate." Understanding the meanings of "relate," "correlate," and "coordinate" makes an understanding of the relationship of these words clearer.

A family vacation may be used to illustrate the meaning of these terms. A mother, father, and teen-age son are getting ready to go on vacation. These family members are related. They share a common origin and a common heritage. But being related as a family does not mean that they are always correlated as a family because the meaning of correlation is to relate together. When the family decides to take a vacation, however, they are not only related, but also correlated. They relate together to achieve a common goal—vacation. Ordinarily, the daily activities of a father take him to his place of employment. The mother's activities keep her in the home. The son's activities center in school. But when these family members go on vacation, they become related together to accomplish this common purpose. Then, as they relate themselves together around this common purpose, they begin to move in harmonious actions to achieve this purpose. Their actions become coordinated, for coordination means to move in harmonious action. The father makes reservations; the mother checks the tour service for routes; and the son gets the car serviced. All of these actions are necessary before going on vacation. Each task is distinctive, and, yet, all are coordinated into a harmonious pattern of action to reach the goal of taking a vacation together.

The organizations of a church are related. These organizations grow out of the nature, purpose, and functions of a church and exist to perform jobs for a church. But it is possible for church organizations to be related without being correlated. The idea of correlation is to relate the organizations together to accomplish specific goals for the church. The idea of coordination is that the organizations will move together in harmonious action to achieve these goals.

Woman's Missionary Union, one unit of a church program, should be a part of a total correlated and coordinated church program. While Woman's Missionary Union is responsible for carrying out its distinctive tasks, these tasks must always be planned and carried out in relationship to the work being done by other church program organizations.

II. TOGETHER IN THE CHURCH COUNCIL

A church council is the key to a coordinated church program. It is not possible to expect a large group like the congregation to spend the long periods of time required to plan a coordinated program of work for a church. The church council provides the means by which the congregation may be assured that the interests of the total church program are given priority over the interests of the various organizations. Through church council planning, the interests of each organization merge to become the work of a church in its total expression.

The members of a church council are the pastor and church staff, Sunday School superintendent, Training Union director, Woman's Missionary Union president, Brotherhood president, and music director (where minister of music is not on church staff). Ex officio members of the council who are expected to attend meetings when matters relating to their work are to be discussed are the following: director of audio-visual education, church librarian, chairmen of church committees, and church officers. The chairman of deacons is on the council either as a regular or as an ex officio member. The pastor serves as chairman of the church council.

1. *The Work of the Council*

The church council is an advisory and coordinating group through which all organizations and committees may coordinate their activities into one harmonious program of work for the church. The council is not an authoritative or administrative group. The congregation makes ultimate decisions. Once the council agrees on a coordinated plan of action and the congregation approves the action, the leader of one of the church organizations or the chairman of a church committee becomes responsible for seeing that the plans are carried out.

A church might depend on its church council to assume the following responsibilities:

(1) Formulate and recommend to the congregation suggested church objectives and goals.
(2) Develop and recommend to the congregation plans of action for reading church goals.
(3) Review and coordinate suggested program plans and actions by church officers, organizations, and committees; and provide for adequate communication among officers, organizations, and committees.
(4) Review and report, as appropriate, to the congregation the use of resources in terms of the needs of church programs as they work toward the achievement of the objectives and goals of a church.
(5) Evaluate program achievements in terms of church objectives and goals, and report evaluations to the congregation.

The success or failure of the church council will be largely determined by the relationship it maintains to all of a church's life. The church council must demonstrate an appreciation for the contribution of each unit of the total church program. There are many groups in a church with which the council must maintain understanding and planning relationships. The council needs to relate properly to the congregation, pastor, church staff, the program organizations, the church officers, and the church committees.

The church council serves as an advisory group to the congregation. It makes recommendations and reports to the congregation within the scope of its assigned tasks. The church council makes no decisions for the congregation unless the congregation specifically empowers it to do so. The congregation might choose to refer program matters that come from the floor during business meetings to the council for study and recommendation before taking official action.

The congregation looks ultimately to the pastor for leadership of the total church program. The church council is a means by which the pastor can lead a church's program. As chairman of the council, the pastor gives leadership at strategic points in the total program. The council provides the pastor with the means for administering the programs of the church. Through the council he can help create an environment in which church leaders can mature.

2. WMU and the Church Council

Woman's Missionary Union is represented on the church council by the WMU president. As a member of the council, she has two major responsibilities: to help develop the best course of action for the church and to represent the organization she leads.

The church council does not have the authority to direct the work of Woman's Missionary Union or any other church organization. The council can suggest and recommend, however, that certain actions be taken by Woman's Missionary Union. The congregation may request Woman's Missionary Union and other church organizations to take specific actions.

The Woman's Missionary Union president has an obligation to the congregation to act in the best interest of the whole church rather than in the interest of her organization should there be a conflict in loyalties between the two. This principle may require that certain ambitions of an organization be relinquished in favor of other activities that are of greater value to the whole church at a particular time. What is most important in the life of a church at a given time is not a decision to be made by one or by a few members; the congregation makes the final decision. Every congregational decision should be made under the leadership of Christ, the head of the church.

The Woman's Missionary Union president serving on the church council gains an appreciation for the work of others and helps other church leaders understand and appreciate the work of the organization she represents. She sees her organization in relationship to the entire church program. In the council she helps engender a spirit of cooperation and involvement which helps motivate a church to action.

Those who work together in the close association of the church council are co-laborers with God and with each other in a church's work. The Woman's Missionary Union president is a vital part of this fellowship among church leaders. In serving on the church council, the Woman's Missionary Union president assists in planning, coordinating, and evaluating the church's work.

A person who is elected to serve as a Woman's Missionary Union president assumes a major leadership responsibility in a church. A church looks to this leader as being responsible for leading the WMU to perform its tasks. The church expects this leader to think comprehensively about church needs. The president is responsible for leading Woman's Missionary Union to help coordinate the program of a church. Such responsibility makes participation on the church council essential.

III. TOGETHER IN THE WMU COUNCIL

In a church, the church council coordinates the work. In Woman's Missionary Union, the WMU Council (Executive Board) coordinates the work. The WMU president gives leadership to the WMU Council. Serving with her on the Council are other WMU officers, WMS presidents, YWA director, GA director, and Sunbeam Band director.

The WMU Council may meet monthly or quarterly to

carry on its work. For most effective results, it is recommended that the Council meet monthly.

The work of the WMU Council may be organized around three major functions: plan, coordinate, and evaluate.

1. Plan
   (1) Make broad plans for carrying out the church tasks assigned to WMU.
   (2) Plan WMU actions designed to help the church reach its goals.
   (3) Make definite work assignments for each action planned.
   (4) Review plans and coordinate with plans of other church organizations.
   (5) Schedule activities on church calendar.
   (6) Plan for resources (such as leadership, finances, facilities) needed to carry out the WMU program.

2. Coordinate
   (1) Coordinate all WMU plans involving more than one age-level WMU organization.
   (2) Coordinate special church projects, such as church observance of Weeks of Prayer, mission offerings, mission study, and mission action.
   (3) Coordinate plans involving discovery of prospects, new units, meeting times and meeting places, and equipment.
   (4) Coordinate enlistment and training of workers.
   (5) Coordinate use of facilities.
   (6) Coordinate budget or financial planning.
   (7) Coordinate relationships among WMU organizations and with other church organizations.

3. Evaluate
   (1) Evaluate the work of WMU in light of the church's objectives and goals.
   (2) Evaluate progress of the WMU program.
   (3) Evaluate plans and projects of each age-level organization; suggest adjustments as necessary.

The WMU Council is a key to the efficient and effective functioning of a Woman's Missionary Union organization in a church. This planning and coordinating group can keep

Woman's Missionary Union aware of its purposes, busy fulfilling its tasks in the life of a church, and properly related to the total program of work in a church.

Beyond the broad planning done by the WMU Council, each WMU age-level organization has its own planning group which plans the work of that unit organization.

IV. TOGETHER AS LEADERS IN A MISSIONS TASK

If a Woman's Missionary Union measures up to its responsibilities in a church, it must have adequate leadership.

How does a leader develop? Election may thrust upon a person the title of leader, but leadership skills come through study and practice.

Successful leaders estimate that 10 percent of their success is due to technical competence or knowing what to do, and 90 percent is due to knowing how to work with others. Certain qualities of leaders should characterize those who serve through Woman's Missionary Union.

1. *Sense of Purpose*

Someone said, "The world stands aside to let a person pass who knows where he is going." An awareness of purpose consistently points a leader in the right direction. When a leader understands organizational purposes and the members' relationship to them, he is laying a strong foundation on which he can build leadership skills.

Leaders in Woman's Missionary Union should feel the impelling force of missionary responsibility in Christ's commission. They should sense the significant place WMU has in helping its members express missions concern and in assisting a church to fulfil its missionary task. The belief in these deeper purposes of WMU brings meaning to meetings and planning.

Purposes must not only be understood but also communicated. A leader reveals his sense of purpose by what he does more than by what he says. Enthusiasm grows out of a sense of purpose and makes it possible for a leader to react with eagerness and anticipation. The leader's capacity for generating excitement about ideas and events is the mark of a leader whose sense of purpose is consuming.

2. *Willingness to Learn*

Leadership techniques and methods are constantly changing. The "why" of Woman's Missionary Union work remains constant, but the "what" and the "how" are always new. A prime requisite for a leader is willingness to learn. By persistent study and careful listening, the leader can add to his information and increase his ability to understand, interpret, evaluate, and lead. Only those leaders who have stopped learning stand still.

3. *Realistic Attitude*

Nearly everyone engages in wishful thinking from time to time. But constant daydreaming can impair a leader's ability to think realistically. Problems are not solved by turning away and thinking how pleasant it would be without them. An unpleasant relationship with a co-worker will not disappear by ignoring it. Failing to face reality in one situation only makes it more difficult in the next.

Realistic thinking is valuable in ways other than solving problems. When persons are being chosen who will assist the leader with her tasks, realistic thinking is necessary. A leader who can accurately evaluate the abilities of another and enlist her in the place of service which will help develop her potential shows clear and realistic thinking. This kind of judgment requires awareness and sensitivity. There are always dimensions of human personality and ability which only the discerning leader can see. Final judgment must be based not only on what a person is but also on what a person can become.

4. Flexibility

Flexibility is responding to and adjusting quickly to new developments and changed situations. Inflexibility implies rigidity and unyielding attitudes. Methods in older and more established organizations are difficult to change, but one mark of a leader is the ability to evaluate change and to incorporate worthy ideas into an organization. Progress necessitates change. Leaders are responsible for guiding persons and organizations in progressive ways.

Leaders in Woman's Missionary Union need to be flexible and able to evaluate change. The creative leader is flexible. New ideas are welcomed, thought through, adapted as necessary, and tried. Even an accidental change in plans is used to advantage, just as a sculptor's chisel may slip and produce a striking, although unintended, effect.

5. Integrity

People admire leaders and tend to place implicit trust in them. A leader is usually looked up to, respected, and admired. Only a leader with sound moral judgment, impeccable character, and Christian dedication is worthy of trust.

"We can trust her" and "She keeps her promise" are words which indicate that followers feel their interests are safe in the hands of their leader, for their leader has integrity.

When followers lose confidence in a leader, it is not usually for major transgressions but for minor, even subtle, inconsistencies which eat at the heart of effectiveness.

6. Dedication to God

The best and most inclusive characteristic of a leader is dedication. Dedication to God provides the motive for effective service. It provides the source of strength and confidence for all tasks. What a person cannot do alone can be done with God's help.

When Christ enlisted people in his service, he often said, "Come ye after me, and I will make you to become . . ." (Mark 1:17). A leader in Woman's Missionary Union does not serve WMU; she serves Christ through his church. Because of this role, there is no substitute for loyalty to God and dedication to his purposes.

A right relationship to God will help the leader relate properly to those led. The leader needs a genuine concern for individuals. This concern will enable the leader to understand persons and to discover ways to meet individual needs. A leader who works well with others can help persons release their best abilities and efforts into the work being done.

> "I cannot lead,
>   dear Lord," I said;
> "I cannot see
>   the way ahead."
> "You do not need
>   to see," said he;
> "Just walk with them,
>   and walk with me." [1]
>
> MARJORIE LOU STUMP

V. LABORING FOR THE FUTURE

Today's world seems to describe all of life with superlatives. Everything is the biggest, fastest, most, worst, or best that has ever been. Superlatives also characterize conversations about Woman's Missionary Union. These are the days of big plans, best opportunities, greatest challenge, and most worthy goals.

These are also days of change. The very effective television advertisement reminds us that the swish, swish of the old washing machine has given way to the smooth hum of the automatic washer. The horse and buggy combination, wonderful in its day, is a hazard on today's superhighway; but the jerky old washing machine and the horse and buggy paved the way for better days.

Progress demands new ways.

Fannie E. S. Heck, a former president of Woman's Missionary Union, said in a president's message in 1909: "The pages of history are strewn with wrecks of organizations which died of inflexibility. . . . It would be possible for Woman's Missionary Union to so tread in old paths that it might outlive its usefulness and be justly numbered with the things of the past. Here is a demand for the highest statesmanship. A knowledge of changing conditions, the foresight to lead rather than be driven, to seize and mold rather than complain and retard progress. Such statesmanship requires a dispassionate consideration of every method however honored, solely on its merits and its discontinuance for a better and broader one, just so soon as it has ceased to fulfil its mission. This by no means seeks to exalt the new, simply because it is new, to veer with every passing fad in missions or in methods, but constantly to have an open mind and a progressive outlook and try both old and new on the keenest edge of our clearest judgment, to give to God's affairs the same long and careful forethought that we would to our own and, with that caution which is a woman's characteristic, fit the instrument to the accomplishment."

The past is past. Old ways of doing work have changed, but some of the spirit of Miss Heck and of Woman's Missionary Union in 1909 could profitably be the spirit of Woman's Missionary Union today. Her phrase "a knowledge of changing conditions, the foresight to lead rather than be driven, to seize and mold" is as contemporary as the present. Woman's Missionary Union must remain flexible and face each opportunity with open-mindedness and frank objectivity.

"Business as usual" will not accomplish the task of the

church in today's world. Changes are necessary to meet the demands of a new age. The nature of the children of God and the body of Christ will not change. The work which Christ commissioned his church to do will not change. But the demands on a church, imposed by its environment, will change, and methods and procedures must change to equip a church to be and to do what Christ intends.

The continuing task of Woman's Missionary Union in a church is to teach missions and to engage members in participation in missions at home and abroad. In helping a church fulfil the mission for which Christ established it, Woman's Missionary Union works closely with all other church organizations and with the pastor and church staff. Within the fellowship of the church, Woman's Missionary Union can discover new meaning in its watchword: "Laborers together with God."

References

Chapter 1

1. *Foreign Mission Journal*, Vol. 19, No. 5 (December, 1887), p. 1.
2. Alma Hunt, *Woman's Missionary Union* (Birmingham: Woman's Missionary Union, 1960), p. 10.
3. Courts Redford, "A Woman's Love," *Home Missions* (January, 1963), p. 4.
4. *The Baptist Program* (September, 1958), p. 24.

Chapter 2

1. Mildred McMurry, *Educating Youth in Missions* (Nashville: Convention Press, 1960), pp. 65–66.
2. J. B. Lawrence, *Missions in the Bible* (Atlanta: Home Mission Board, 1931), p. 15.
3. Mildred McMurry, *Educating Youth in Missions* (Nashville: Convention Press, 1960), pp. 104, 106.
4. Alma Hunt, *Woman's Missionary Union* (Birmingham: Woman's Missionary Union, 1960), p. 28.

Chapter 3

1. Billie Pate, "I Saw Need Today," *The Window* (March, 1960).
2. Helen Fling, *Enlistment for Missions* (Nashville: Convention Press, 1962), p. 133. Used by permission.
3. Vernon Elmore, "What Is a Missionary Dollar?" *The Baptist Program* (April, 1962), p. 34.
4. Hugo Culpepper, "Whither Southern Baptist Missions?" *Review and Expositor*, LXII (Winter, 1965), p. 5.

Chapter 4

1. Baker James Cauthen, "Why Lottie Moon Offering Is Vital," *The Commission* (November, 1957), p. 9.

Chapter 5

1. Marjorie Lou Stump, *Church Administration* (1961).

Suggestions for the Teacher

How in the world do I start? This may be your biggest question at the moment. The answer is, Keep reading. Read all the book at one sitting. Read all the teaching helps. Realize that planning saves time.

Participation by members of the group will be a key to the success of each session. A number of things may be done to help secure participation.

1. Remember that the room teaches. Arrange the chairs in a circle, semicircle, or V. If the group is small, remain seated as you teach. This makes you a part of the group.
2. Have available for each session all the materials suggested. If you are using learning aids, be sure you can use them effectively.
3. Refuse to be an authority. When a question is asked, turn it back to the group by saying: "What do the rest of you think?"
4. Provide opportunity for working in small groups.
5. Use "Before the Session" as your checklist.
6. After each session, evaluate what was done.

Chapter 1

Study Question: Historically and presently, how does WMU help a church become aware of its missions responsibilities?

BEFORE THE SESSION

- ☐ On newsprint or poster board, write the title of the book and the chapter titles.
- ☐ Assign to a member the "Introduction."
- ☐ Write on newsprint the study question.
- ☐ Write each task on a strip of paper. Tack these up as called for in "During the Session."

DURING THE SESSION

1. If members of the group do not know one another, ask each to tell her name and something about herself.

2. Using the newsprint, preview the content of the book. Outline briefly the content of each chapter.
3. Read the study question for this session from the newsprint. Place it in front of the group for the rest of the session.
4. Ask the person assigned the "Introduction" to give her report.
5. Ask for a definition of "church." Write it on the chalkboard and discuss it. Compare it with the definition in this chapter. Ask: What are key phrases in the definition? Discuss.
6. Ask someone to read aloud the tasks of WMU. Place each task on the wall in front of the group. Say: The study of these tasks will be the basic study of this book. Check the statement of tasks against chapter titles to show that chapters discuss tasks.
7. Divide into five small groups. Assign to each group one of the five basic beliefs regarding a church and missions. Ask each group to discuss the belief for six minutes. Allow about two minutes each for reports.

CHAPTER 2

Study Question: What is the meaning of the task Teach missions?

BEFORE THE SESSION

☐ On poster board print the three areas of content for teaching missions.
☐ Reproduce the chart showing relationships (see p. 117).
☐ Prepare a time line. (See point 3 under "During the Session.")
☐ Write the study question on newsprint.

DURING THE SESSION

1. Read the study question. Place it in front of the group for this session.
2. Discuss learning and learners.
3. Using the poster board, refer to the first area of content for teaching missions. Ask a member to give examples from the Old Testament and from the New Testament which show God's redemptive acts.
4. Tack up the words Teach Missions. Discuss the role of the Holy Spirit in missions. (This was called for in the first session.)

5. Refer to the second area of content. Review this section by using this time line.

X	X	X	X	X	X
Early Christians	Middle Ages	Reformation	1800s	1845	Present

6. Refer to the third area of content: contemporary missions. Discuss content of this section.
7. Ask members to share their ideas of the importance of teaching missions and testimonies of teaching missions in their homes.
8. Using the chart showing relationships, explain the relationship of WMU to other church program organizations in the task of teaching missions.

CHAPTER 3

Study Question: How may members of WMU become involved in missions?

BEFORE THE SESSION

☐ Write the study question on newsprint.
☐ Assign in advance the section "A Church Responds to the World."

DURING THE SESSION

1. Read the study question and place it before the group.
2. Ask for the report from the person assigned "A Church Responds to the World."
3. Explain the task: Lead persons to participate in missions. Tack the strip with this task on it below "Teach missions." (This was called for in chapter 1.)
4. Ask the group to list as rapidly as possible all the ways they can think of in which a person may become involved in missions. Ask someone to record these on the chalkboard. Lead the group to discuss the ways they consider to be most vital. Most of the content of this chapter can be discussed as these ideas are ranked.
5. Refer to the relationship chart as you discuss relationships with other church program organizations.

CHAPTER 4

Study Question: What is the full meaning of the tasks concerning projects and channeling?

BEFORE THE SESSION

☐ Write the study question on newsprint.

DURING THE SESSION

1. Place before the group the study question for this session.
2. Tack in place the strip stating the projects task. (This was called for in chapter 1.)
3. Ask someone to define the word "project." Discuss characteristics of projects.
4. Ask: Which projects are most familiar to WMU members? When discussing the Lottie Moon Christmas Offering and the Annie Armstrong Offering, give the total amount of the offering for the current year. Discuss the total amount given by your church to each offering. Lead the group to discover the balance between these amounts, the amount kept by the church, and the amount sent through the Cooperative Program.
5. Ask members to share experiences from prayer retreats, weeks of prayer, and special prayer meetings.
6. Place in order the strip of paper on which the channeling task is written. Read it. (This was called for in chapter 1.)
7. Using examples in the chapter, show how WMU may interpret the work of the church and the denomination.

CHAPTER 5

Study Question: What evidences are there that leaders must work together if WMU is to accomplish its tasks?

BEFORE THE SESSION

☐ Write on newsprint the study question.
☐ Assign in advance the family illustration explaining coordination and correlation.
☐ Assign in advance to the president a discussion of the church council.
☐ Assign in advance to an age-group director a report on the WMU Council.

DURING THE SESSION

1. Ask members to say the first thing that comes to their mind when you say the word "together." Probably the WMU watchword will be mentioned. Build on this to show the meaning of the word to the total program of a church.

2. Place before the group the newsprint stating the study question.
3. Ask for the report on the family vacation.
4. Ask the president to discuss the church council. If your church does not have a functioning council, ask the group to suggest ways one might be set up.
5. Ask the age-group director to discuss the work of the WMU Council. As each function is discussed, write it on the chalkboard: planning, coordinating, evaluating.
6. Ask the group to list characteristics they think are basic in leaders if WMU is to accomplish its tasks. Check these against the list in this chapter, and discuss.
7. Give to each member paper and pencil. Ask each to write a paragraph stating the future of WMU as she understands it in light of the concepts presented in this study.

For Review and Written Work

1. What is the biblical basis for a church's mission?
2. What is the scope of a church's missions task?
3. What is the meaning of the word "organization"?
4. To what were women responding when Woman's Missionary Union came into being?
5. What tasks does WMU perform for a church?
6. What are the five basic beliefs about a church and missions?

CHAPTER 2

1. State the teaching task of Woman's Missionary Union.
2. What is the content of the task: Teach missions?
3. Why is teaching missions important?
4. Teaching missions is one part of the total educational curriculum of a church. State in a brief paragraph WMU's relationship to the following church program organizations in teaching missions:
    (1) Brotherhood
    (2) Sunday School
    (3) Training Union
    (4) Music Ministry

CHAPTER 3

1. Since learning is intended to result in action, what should be a person's response to learning about missions?
2. What should be the response when a Christian looks at conditions in the world?
3. Explain the meaning of the task: Lead persons to participate in missions.
4. List the three major areas of opportunity for participation in missions, and write a sentence describing each.
5. Write a paragraph summarizing WMU's relationship to other church program organizations in the task of leading persons to participate in missions.

CHAPTER 4

1. List the characteristics of special projects.
2. What are some of the projects for which WMU can provide organization and leadership?
3. Define the channeling task.
4. How may WMU interpret the work of a church?
5. How may WMU interpret the work of the denomination?

CHAPTER 5

1. What is meant by correlation and coordination?
2. What seems to be the key to a coordinated church program?
3. How is WMU represented on the church council?
4. List the three major functions of the WMU Council.
5. What characteristics of leaders seem necessary if WMU accomplishes a church's missions task?
6. Write any new understandings you have gained from this study.
7. State your commitment to the missions task as you relate to your church.

Appendix

Basic Materials for Conducting the WMU Program of a Church

WMU Yearbook

Issued yearly, this book contains dated emphases and plans for Woman's Missionary Union in a church.

CURRICULUM AND LEADERSHIP MAGAZINES

Royal Service

This monthly magazine for WMS leaders and members contains study materials, guides for individual and group participation in missions, and a leadership insert of how-to suggestions for leaders.

The Window

This magazine brings curriculum materials and program suggestions to YWA members and leaders monthly.

Tell

Junior and Intermediate GA members use *Tell* monthly to guide the activities of their organization. A leadership edition of *Tell* brings assistance to GA directors and counselors in their work.

Sunbeam Activities

This magazine, published quarterly, carries units of study for Sunbeam Bands and helps for Sunbeam Band leaders.

LEADERSHIP MANUALS

There is a leadership manual for each WMU age-level organization:

Woman's Missionary Society Manual
Young Woman's Auxiliary Manual
Girl's Auxiliary Leadership Guide
Primary Sunbeam Band Manual for Leaders

Beginner Sunbeam Band Manual for Leaders
The Sunbeam Nursery

(The magazines may be ordered from Woman's Missionary Union, 600 North 20th Street, Birmingham, Alabama 35203. Other materials are available from the same source or from your Baptist Book Store.)

Church Tasks Performed by Church Program Organizations

	Sunday School	Brotherhood	WMU	Training Union	Music Ministry
Teaching	Teach the biblical revelation [1]	Teach missions [1]	Teach missions [1]	Teach systematic theology, Christian history, Christian ethics, and church polity and organization [1]	Teach music and hymnody [1]
Outreach	Lead in reaching all prospects for the church [4]	Lead all men, young men, and boys to participate in mission activities	Teach missions [2] → Lead persons to participate in missions [3]	Give orientation to new church members [5]	Provide music and musicians for congregational services and organizations of the church [9]
Performance of Functions	Lead all church members to worship, witness, learn, and minister daily [6]			Train church members to worship, witness, learn, and minister daily [7]	Lead persons to participate in hymn singing [9]
Training				Discover, recruit, and train potential leaders [8]	Train persons to lead, sing, and play music [9]
Special Projects	[10] Provide organization and leadership for special projects of the church				
Channeling	[11] Provide and interpret information regarding the work of the church and denomination				

WMU Tasks in Relationship to the Tasks of Other Church Organizations

(The chart shows the tasks performed by church program organizations. The arrows show relationship of WMU tasks to the tasks of other church organizations. Numbers on the chart correspond to the number used in this explanation of relationships.)

1. The first task in each organization is a teaching task. All organizations are engaged in teaching, but the content to be taught by each is different. WMU and Brotherhood share the distinctive task of teaching missions.

2. The other tasks of WMU grow out of its teaching task. Because WMU teaches missions, all other activities of the organization are related to missions.

3. Participation in missions includes praying for missions, giving to missions, and witnessing and ministering through mission action.

4. Sunday School has the task of reaching all prospects for the church. WMU supplements and supports the outreach activities of Sunday School through mission action in the community. The Sunday School brings prospects directly to the church. WMU ministers to persons of special need or circumstance in the community who are not immediate prospects for the church, with the intention of ultimately reaching them for Christ and the church.

5. As WMU reaches people for membership in the church through mission action, the Training Union stands ready to give these new church members orientation. From this training center provided by Training Union, new church members are sent out to serve through the many avenues of opportunity in the church.

6. The Sunday School, based on its Bible teaching, leads all church members to worship, witness, learn, and minister daily. WMU, based on the teaching of missions, leads persons to participate in missions. The actions of WMU add dimension to the actions of Sunday School. For example, while Sunday

School is leading all church members to worship daily, WMU is leading persons to pray for missions as a part of this worship experience. And while Sunday School is leading all church members to witness and minister daily, WMU is conducting mission action in the community to relate witness and ministry to people of special need or circumstance.

7. In addition to new member orientation, Training Union gives training to all church members. This training will help build the skills WMU members need to perform the tasks WMU carries out for the church.

8. The Training Union discovers, recruits, and trains potential leaders. As some of these potential leaders actually assume WMU leadership positions, WMU provides specialized training in the principles and methods of WMU work to supplement the basic training in Training Union.

9. Music is a vital part of WMU. The Music Ministry assists WMU by training musicians to lead music for WMU meetings, and by encouraging and training persons to participate in hymn singing.

10. The special projects task is common to all organizations. It means that the organizations stand ready to do any special job the church wants done. WMU will carry out projects for the church related to missions.

11. In the last task, each organization serves as a channel of communication for the church and denomination. WMU will keep its members informed about and involved in the work of the church and denomination.

Some Significant Events in the History of
Woman's Missionary Union

1800–1811—Societies for the promotion of missions by women and children began to emerge.

1812—The Wadmalaw and Edisto Female Mite Society of South Carolina contributed $122.50 to missions.

1813—Following the return of Luther Rice to America in 1813 to promote the support of foreign missions, missionary societies for women and children sprang up rapidly.

1817—The 1817 Triennial Convention listed reports from 110 women's societies.

1832—Female mission societies were organized in most southern states.

1835—Appointment of the J. Lewis Shucks of Virginia by the Board of the Triennial Convention to serve in China further stimulated the missionary interest and activity of women in the South.

1840—The Triennial Convention gave special recognition to the contributions of women's societies.

1845—Southern Baptist Convention was organized in Augusta, Georgia.

1868—Mrs. Ann Graves, mother of R. H. Graves, missionary to China, called together women attending the Southern Baptist Convention in Baltimore for a meeting in the basement of the church to relate information about missions and to pray for missions. This is considered to be the first general meeting of Southern Baptist women in the interest of missions.

1871—Baptist women of Baltimore organized a federation of Baptist women's societies known as "Woman's Mission to Woman."

1872—The Southern Baptist Convention for the first time appointed a Committee on Women's Work and approved its report, including a recommendation that the delegates present at the Southern Baptist Convention "take immediate steps to organize Female Missionary Societies in their churches."

1873—The Foreign Mission Board appointed Lottie Moon to join her sister Edmonia in China.

1875—A state central committee was formed in South Carolina "to arouse an interest in the work among the women of the state and secure contributions." By 1876, H. A. Tupper, Foreign Mission Board secretary, was influential in the organization of central committees for women's work in most of the states.

1877—The Southern Baptist Convention appointed a Committee on Women's Work for Home Missions. The Southern Baptist Convention Committee on Woman's Work for Foreign Missions stated that "the time may be at hand" when it will be advisable that the women "shall appoint a Central Committee to combine their efforts, to stimulate the work, and to give permanent record to their success."

1880—The Forward Movement Committee of the Southern Baptist Convention commended the work of Woman's Missionary Societies and urged the organization of such societies in every church.

1887—Lottie Moon wrote an article, published in the *Foreign Mission Journal* in December, expressing the conviction that organization of Southern Baptist women was "the imperative need of the hour," suggesting the structure or organization and stating that a week of prayer and an offering at Christmas would give unity and purpose to the organization.

1888—Women delegates, appointed by twelve states, met simultaneously with the Southern Baptist Convention in Richmond, Virginia. The delegates adopted a constitution and formed an organization called the "Executive Committee of the Woman's Mission Societies (Auxiliary to Southern Baptist Convention)." They selected Baltimore as headquarters for the new organization and elected Annie Armstrong as corresponding secretary.

1889—The Southwide Woman's Missionary Society voted to continue the special Christmas offering for missions in China; also to continue the special offering for home mission work in Cuba. The plan of work adopted by the Woman's Missionary Society called for the organization of associational and district committees to promote the formation of societies in the churches. They were to hold quarterly and annual meetings for inspirational and promotional purposes.

1890—The organization changed its name to Woman's Missionary Union, Auxiliary to the Southern Baptist Convention.

1891—The Convention endorsed the Sunbeam movement and commended the work of the women's societies with the children.

1892—The Convention commended the Woman's Missionary Union for its work during the last five years and for the women's contributions to missions, which totaled over $44,000 during the past year.

In January Woman's Missionary Union sponsored a South-wide week of prayer for the cause of the Centennial movement. The Southern Baptist Convention approved and commended the plan devised by the Woman's Missionary Union for using chapel cards and certificates in the effort to raise money for the Centennial Fund.

1894—The Sunday School Board agreed to take charge of promoting Missionary Day in the Sunday Schools, with the assistance of Woman's Missionary Union.

1895—The Southern Baptist Convention Committee on Women's Work commended the Woman's Missionary Union for its effectiveness and its loyalty to the Convention.

1896—Responsibility for promotion of Sunbeam work, under the direction of George Braxton Taylor, since its beginning, was transferred by the Foreign Mission Board to Woman's Missionary Union.

The recommendation of the Home Board that the Woman's Missionary Union observe the Week of Self-Denial, in the interest of home missions, was adopted by the Union.

1901—The $3,500 raised by Woman's Missionary Union for the Church Building Loan Fund of the Home Board provided the foundation for the initiation of this work by the Board.

1907—Woman's Missionary Union approved the name Young Woman's Auxiliary for the young women's societies functioning in the churches.

1908—The name "Royal Ambassador Chapters" was given to the mission organization for boys.

1910—Woman's Missionary Union reported cooperation with the Laymen's Movement in initiating the latter's plans for missionary advance in the churches.

The objectives of Woman's Missionary Union were broadened to include personal service work.

1913—By Convention action the previous year, Woman's Missionary Union made its first direct report to the Southern Baptist Convention. The report was read by W. O. Carver. Heretofore, Woman's Missionary Union had made its annual report through the Home and Foreign Mission Boards.

1914—The name "Girls' Auxiliary" was adopted for the mission organization for girls.

The Southern Baptist Convention endorsed the report of its Committee on Women's Work, which called on Southern Baptists to recognize "the Woman's Missionary Union as one of the greatest educational forces enlisted in the cause of missions."

Our Mission Fields became a thirty-two page monthly magazine called *Royal Service*.

1915—Woman's Missionary Union commended the "personal service" conducted by the Women's Societies throughout the Convention territory, including such activities and projects as rescue work, good will centers, Homemaker's clubs, industrial schools, Vacation Bible School work, mission Sunday Schools, work with Negroes, work with foreigners.

1918—Southern Baptist Convention revised its constitution to insert the word "messengers" for the word "brethren," thus making it possible for women to be messengers to the Convention.

1919—The Southern Baptist Convention adopted recommendations that Southern Baptists enter a campaign to raise $75,000,000 during the next five years for the Convention's work. Woman's Missionary Union took as its quota $15,-000,000.

1921—Woman's Missionary Union requested representation of women on Southern Baptist Convention Boards and Executive Committee.

Woman's Missionary Union headquarters moved from Baltimore to Birmingham.

1924—Woman's Missionary Union continued to emphasize the following aims: Individual and United Prayer, Bible Study, Soul-winning, Enlistment, Mission Study, Organized Personal Service, and Systematic and Proportionate Giving.

1925—The total gifts of Woman's Missionary Union to the 75

Million Campaign amounted to $16,713,100 (redeemed original pledge of $15,000,000).

Woman's Missionary Union voted to launch a stewardship campaign to enlist more tithers among its own members and the church membership at large.

The Cooperative Program came into being. The Convention action stated that the launching of the Cooperative Program was "in no way to interfere with . . . weeks of prayer of the Woman's Missionary Union" and that "the special thank-offerings for state and home missions and the Christmas offering for foreign missions ingathered during the Week of Prayer of the Woman's Missionary Union for these respective causes shall be recognized as gifts in addition to the regular contributions to the Cooperative Program."

1938—The Woman's Missionary Union president was appointed to serve on the Southern Baptist Convention Committee on Coordination and Correlation.

1949—The Southern Baptist Convention Inter-Agency Council was formed, consisting of representatives of Woman's Missionary Union and other agencies "for the purpose of coordinating and correlating plans, programs, activities, materials, objectives, so far as may be needful and practicable, before sending them out to the churches."

1950—Membership in Woman's Missionary Union organizations passed the one million mark.

1954—Royal Ambassador work was transferred from Woman's Missionary Union to Brotherhood with the stipulation that the Royal Ambassador program continue to be a missionary organization.

1958—The Southern Baptist Convention approved the recommendation made by the Committee on Total Program that Woman's Missionary Union should be continued as an auxiliary to the Southern Baptist Convention, that Woman's Missionary Union should continue to perform its present functions, and that the work of Woman's Missionary Union should be related to that of the Southern Baptist Convention agencies through the Inter-Agency Council.

1963—Woman's Missionary Union observed its 75th Anniversary. The Southern Baptist Convention adopted a resolution commending the work of Woman's Missionary Union in support of the Convention.

Relationship of Mission Action
to Study

Following through on the study of missions should prompt WMU members to witness and minister in three ways: (1) spontaneous response to witnessing and ministering opportunities, (2) participation in other witnessing and ministering plans of the church, and (3) participation in planned mission action.

1. *Spontaneous Response to Witnessing and Ministering Opportunities*

The study of missions should make all WMU members aware of the needs of people, particularly the need of persons to know Christ as personal Saviour. If the learning experience is truly effective, members will proclaim in their homes and community the message of salvation and will minister to the basic needs of persons in the name of Jesus Christ. The spontaneous response of Christians to the persons with whom they have contact is perhaps the highest expression of missionary concern. This spontaneous expression is the foundation on which planned activities rest. The most effective planned activity takes place when concerned individuals work together.

Spontaneous response to witnessing and ministering opportunities is not confined to persons of special need or circumstance. This kind of response extends itself to all persons with whom the Christian has contact.

2. *Participation in Other Witness and Ministry Plans of the Church*

Study experiences in WMU will also help motivate members to participate in the witness and ministry plans structured by other organizations or planned by the pastor. The Sunday School is responsible for leading in reaching prospects for the church and for leading persons to witness and minister daily. Through the specific plans of Sunday School and general evangelism plans of the church, WMU members will find many opportunities to witness and minister.

3. Participation in Planned Mission Action

While the individual has many opportunities for missionary action growing out of his spontaneous response to the needs of persons, he must also see his responsibilities which can best be expressed as he relates to others in planned activities.

In the task Lead persons to participate in missions Woman's Missionary Union assumes responsibility for guiding involvement in mission action. This implies structuring a mission action program through which people may become participants. It implies both individual and group action.

Mission action in WMU organizations can be conducted in two ways: (1) as an ongoing activity extending over a long period of time, and (2) as a project-type activity, which is short-term. At the young people's and the adult age-levels the ongoing activity is usually the better approach, with projects supporting the ongoing activity. At younger age-levels the project approach is used almost exclusively.

4. Summary

The relationship of mission action to study can be shown with a visual illustration (illustration 1). The ongoing work of teaching missions can be shown with one line. This activity is unending. Leading persons to participate in missions can be shown with a second line. This activity, like teaching missions, goes on all the time.

Illustration 1

Leading Persons to Participate in Missions
_____
(Mission Action)

Teaching Missions
_____
(Study)

Another line can be drawn growing out of study showing the spontaneous response persons will be encouraged to make to witness and ministry opportunities, and to show participation of persons in other witness and ministry plans of the church (illustration 2). Woman's Missionary Union creates an environment through study which helps motivate witnessing and ministering, but the nature of the action is primarily determined by the individual.

It is hoped that spontaneous witness and ministry by individual members and participation in other church plans will be a continuing activity on the part of these persons.

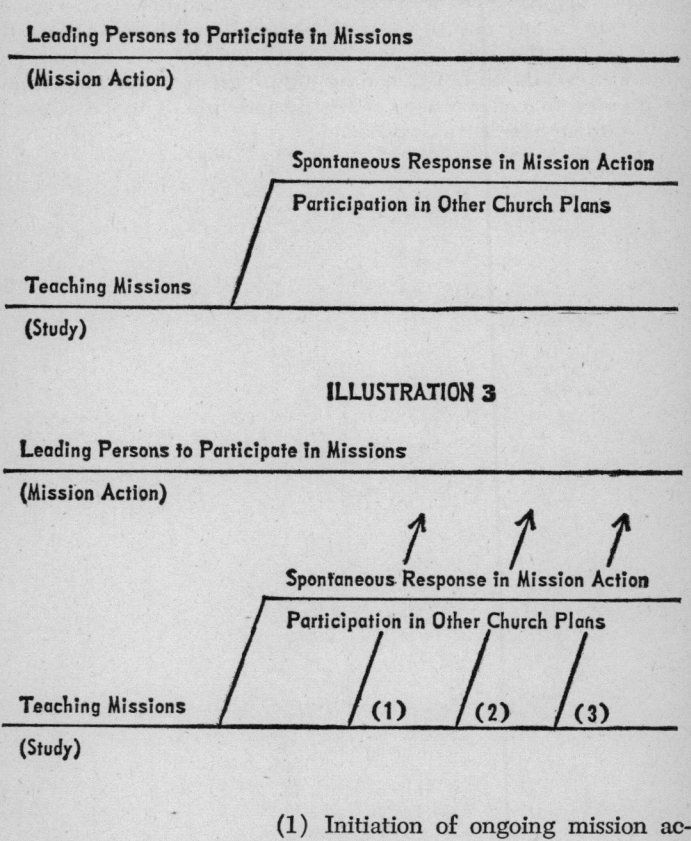

ILLUSTRATION 2

Leading Persons to Participate in Missions

(Mission Action)

Spontaneous Response in Mission Action

Participation in Other Church Plans

Teaching Missions

(Study)

ILLUSTRATION 3

Leading Persons to Participate in Missions

(Mission Action)

Spontaneous Response in Mission Action

Participation in Other Church Plans

Teaching Missions   (1)   (2)   (3)

(Study)

(1) Initiation of ongoing mission action
(2) New thrust or impetus to existing work
(3) Initiation of mission action project

Study also contributes in three distinctive ways to the ongoing mission action program (illustration 3): (1) learning experiences may lead an organization to initiate mission action work; (2) study may give new thrust or impetus to mission action work already being done; (3) study may cause an organization to initiate a short-term project in mission action. As the study experience contributes in any one of these three ways to mission action, it makes use of the spontaneous response persons are making to community needs. In fact, a continuing program of mission action presupposes that there are concerned individuals to be related together to get specific jobs done.

Date Due